ACKNOWLEDGMENTS

My sincere gratitude is warmly ▮▮▮▮▮ ▮▮a Ramon and her children Assaf, Tal, David, and ▮ —for their cooperation made this book possible. While they are indeed living through a very sad time in their lives, they were both gracious and brave to have supported my telling of Ilan's story.

I am equally grateful to Eliezer Wolfermann (Ilan's father) and his cousins, Yael and Evelyn Sucher, for providing stories and photographs of Ilan for this book. Their kind words and thoughts about Ilan will no doubt touch all who read about his life.

I would also like to thank Dr. Ellen Frankel and the Editorial Committee at the Jewish Publication Society for their support in bringing this important biography into the hands of so many young readers. I'm thankful, too, to Carol Hupping, Janet Liss, and Robin Norman at JPS for their excellent editing and production help.

I am most grateful to Professor Reuven Segev (a friend of Ilan's from high school) for his stories and memories, and Rabbi Daniel Gordis for talking to me about his personal friendship with Ilan. And thank you, too, to Rabbi Michael Graetz for all his kind efforts. Thank you, Joel Newberger, for avionics assistance and all things military and mathematical, and to Ilanit Kamin-Newberger for all translating.

I would also like to thank the following people and organizations for providing photographs for this book: The Ramon Family, Eliezer Wolfermann, Michal Roche-Ben Ami from Tel Aviv University, NASA, the National Outdoor Leadership School, the Israel Defense Force, and the Israel Air Force.

And finally, thank you Adam, Jordy, and Halle Rose for your love and support.

Devra Newberger Speregen

ILAN RAMON
Jewish Star

ILAN RAMON

Jewish Star

DEVRA NEWBERGER SPEREGEN

THE JEWISH PUBLICATION SOCIETY
Philadelphia   2004 • 5764

The Jewish Publication Society
2100 Arch Street, 2nd floor
Philadelphia, PA 19103

Design and Composition by Book Design Studio II

Manufactured in the United States of America

04 05 06 07 08 09 10   10 9 8 7 6 5 4 3 2 1

CONTENTS

*Publication of this book was made possible
through a generous grant from
The Yvonne and Leslie Pollack Family Foundation*

*This book is dedicated to the fallen crew of **Columbia** STS-107*

and the families and loved ones of

Ilan Ramon, Rick Husband, William McCool, David Brown,

Michael Anderson, Laurel Clark, and Kalpana Chawla.

It is also dedicated to the release of IAF Colonel Ron Arad,

and to the memory of Tonia Kreppel Wolfermann,

Petr Ginz and all those who perished in the Holocaust.

1

Reaching for the Stars

The last morning aboard the space shuttle *Columbia* began in the same way as the fifteen mornings preceding it: with the peace and quiet calm of space interrupted by the sweet sounds of music over the space shuttle radio, beamed up as a special morning wake-up call for the astronauts, courtesy of NASA's Mission Control in Houston. On this morning—the last morning of the sixteen-day space mission—the seven astronauts aboard *Columbia* were treated to "Scotland the Brave," performed by the band of the 51st Highland Brigade. The Scottish music was chosen in honor of astronaut Laurel Clark and her Scottish heritage.

The morning before, the crew had risen to the sounds of Israeli singer Yehoram Gaon singing a poem written by Jewish poet Rachel, entitled "Shalom Lach Eretz Nehderet" (Hello, You Wonderful Country). That song had been a special request by the Israeli astronaut, Colonel Ilan Ramon.

The music on this morning, the morning of February 1, 2003, however, was more a formality than a wake-up call. In truth, all seven astronauts aboard *Columbia* were awake

1

long before the Scottish bagpipes began calling to them from across the solar system, as it was their last day in space and there was a lot to be done before the spacecraft could re-enter the Earth's atmosphere and land at the Johnson Space Center in Houston, Texas. The landing procedures would easily take more than six hours to accomplish.

After the music had finished playing, astronaut Laurel Clark greeted her fellow NASA astronauts back in Texas over the ship's satellite radio. "We're ready for our big day up here," she told them. "[We] had a great time in orbit, and [are] really excited to come back home."

On the ground at Cape Canaveral in Florida, everything appeared to be in order, too. The weather conditions were perfect for landing, with temperatures in the low 70s. The families of the seven astronauts had already been taken to the runway and were assembling for their VIP, close-up view of touchdown. The pit crew, too, was in place, ready to guide the shuttle back into its hangar upon landing. At NASA Mission Control, operations were similarly routine.

At 8:53 A.M. a sensor that measures temperature on the left wing suddenly blinked out. This was not alarming because sensors sometimes malfunction. But at 8:56 A.M. Mission Control noticed that other heat sensors in the same area were registering abnormally. Two minutes later, three temperature gauges, embedded in the shuttle's "skin" (the outer body of the spacecraft) on the left flank of the ship, stopped transmitting completely.

Aboard the shuttle, the computerized stabilizer automatically kicked in as it tried to fix the wing's temperature problem. It was unsuccessful. Commander Rick Husband

and Pilot William McCool immediately contacted Mission Control back on Earth. Mission Control responded by radio and asked Husband about another abnormal reading they had just received: the tire pressure on the left main landing gear had just dropped to zero. "Roger," Rick Husband replied to Mission Control. "Uh—"

Before he could finish his message, Rick Husband's voice was suddenly cut off. In fact, at that exact moment, all communication from *Columbia* was severed.

In Houston, Major Charlie Hobaugh repeatedly tried to re-establish contact with the shuttle. "*Columbia*, Houston," he called over the radio. "Com check" (communications check). There was no response. Nothing but static.

Mission Control became eerily quiet, all eyes in the room remained fixed on the large consoles in front of them. They strained to hear any response from Rick Husband and *Columbia* over the radio. But as the minutes ticked by, it became tragically apparent that *Columbia* was gone.

Just fifteen minutes from its planned touchdown, more than 200,000 feet above Texas and under the watchful eye of millions of people worldwide, the space shuttle *Columbia* fatally fell apart, taking with it the lives of its seven brave astronauts. There was, however, one last communication from a member of the crew that miraculously came through just moments before the shuttle's breakup. It was an e-mail message sent back to Earth by Colonel Ilan Ramon to his wife, Rona, and their four children— Assaf, Tal, Yiftach, and Noa—who were, at that moment, assembled with all the other family members of the astronauts waiting for touchdown at Cape Canaveral. Ilan's e-mail message made it home, but sadly, the Jewish astronaut who had made this historic journey into space, didn't. He wrote:

> *Though everything here is astonishing, I can't wait until I see you all. Big hugs to the kids. Ilan.*

All over the world, Jewish people mourned the loss of Colonel Ilan Ramon. Though not the first Jew in space, he was the first Israeli astronaut. While he orbited the Earth for sixteen days, Jewish children and their families followed his mission closely, feeling a deep connection to this charismatic, gentle man. Ilan Ramon left a legacy in the Jewish world by participating in a most visible event, all the while proudly wearing his Judaism and his deep devotion to the State of Israel on his "pumpkin" orange spacesuit sleeve.

The tragedy of the space shuttle *Columbia*, and the death of Ilan Ramon and the six astronauts he traveled with, devastated the world. After his untimely death, many people were eager to learn more about Ilan Ramon. Who was this inspiring, extraordinary man? How did such a devoted Israeli Air Force hero come to find himself orbiting the Earth aboard an American space shuttle, representing an entire Jewish nation?

2

Ilan's Roots

*It's very, very peculiar to be the first Israeli up in space,
especially because of my background. But my background is
[symbolic] of a lot of other Israelis' backgrounds. My mother
is a Holocaust survivor. My father fought for the
independence of Israel, not so long ago. I'm kind of the proof
for them, and for the whole Israeli people, that whatever we
fought for is becoming true.*

Ilan Ramon, January, 2003

Ilan Ramon was a hero in every sense of the word. He
was a brave, compassionate, peaceful, and well-educated
man, and he was exceptionally proud to represent Israel
and Jewish people all over the world on a space mission.
He was the smiling astronaut we watched aboard *Columbia* on our televisions in "real-time," performing somer-
saults in the Spacehab and waving an Israeli flag in the
shuttle cockpit.

Ilan was a strong family man who loved children, evi-
denced by the way he spoke to hundreds of schoolchildren while working on experiments during his space
mission. He talked to them from thousands of miles

above the Earth, describing how he felt "like a butterfly" in zero gravity, and how Israel looked so small and peaceful from way up high in the solar system. He was the astronaut who brought Judaica into space in the form of a Holocaust Torah, a *Kiddush Cup*, and a mezuzah, and demonstrated, for all the world to see, how Jews observe Shabbat and keep kosher.

Ilan did not take this great honor lightly. A close friend of the Ramon family, Rabbi Stuart Federow from Houston, Texas, where Ilan and his family lived during his four years of astronaut training, said that Ilan understood that being the first Israeli astronaut brought with it a great responsibility, not just to Israel, but also to Jews worldwide. Ilan was determined to use his position as an astronaut to teach the whole world about Israel and the Jewish people. For the sixteen days Ilan spent aboard *Columbia*, with his Israeli flag hanging boldly on the cockpit wall, Ilan managed to bring a little bit of Jewish tradition and history to the millions of people who followed the space mission.

Ilan Ramon's own parents embodied the spirit of the creation of Israel, its history and struggle for survival. His father, Eliezer Wolfermann, was born in Germany in 1924. In 1935, when Eliezer was 11 years old, he and his parents, Leo and Rosa, left Germany for Tel Aviv, just at the time when Adolf Hitler began his rise to power. Eliezer and his family were very lucky to leave Germany when they did. Soon after their move to Israel, Adolf Hitler and his Nazi army began gathering the Jewish people of Europe and sending them to death camps. Ilan's mother, Tonia Kreppel, was not so lucky.

Tonia Kreppel was born in Poland in 1929. Both she and her mother—Ilan's grandmother—were sent to

Auschwitz, one of the most horrific of Hitler's death camps. "My grandmother was very sick and almost died," Ilan told a Florida newspaper in an interview before the shuttle launch. "My mother was 16 or 17 years old [when she was sent to Auschwitz] and she insisted on staying with her [mother]."

Tonia and her mother spent a year and a half living under brutal conditions at Auschwitz. It was sometime in 1945 when they were finally liberated from the death camp by the Russians. Sadly, many of Ilan's relatives on his mother's side did not survive the Holocaust.

With no place to go, and no home in Poland to return to, Ilan's mother and grandmother took passage on a ship that was headed for Palestine. Like many ships filled with liberated Jews fleeing Germany and the concentration camps, their ship was turned away as it attempted to dock in Palestine. At that time, in the years before Israel was declared a Jewish State, Palestine was under British rule. Because Great Britain did not want the responsibility of taking in so many Jews, they sent all Jewish refugees to "holding camps" (temporary refugee shelters) they had set up on the Turkish island of Cypress. Ilan's mother and grandmother lived in one of these holding camps in Cypress until 1949. A few months after Israel had proclaimed its independence, they were finally permitted to leave the camp and go to Israel.

Eliezer and Tonia met at Kibbutz Givat Chaim, a Jewish cooperative settlement established in 1933 that was located halfway between Tel Aviv and Haifa. They married in 1949, not long after Tonia's *aliyah* to Israel. They eventually moved to Ramat-Gan, a suburb of Tel Aviv. Eliezer's mother, Rosa, had died from asthma a few years

7

before, in 1945. His father (Ilan's grandfather), Leo, died of cancer in 1954, when Ilan was just a baby.

Ilan was born in Ramat-Gan on June 20, 1954. He was the second son born to Eliezer and Tonia, and he and his older brother, Gadi, spent their early childhood living in a *shikun* (apartment complex) called Rasco. When Ilan was eight, his father took an engineering job and moved his family to the southern town of Beersheva. At the time, Beersheva had a population of about 60,000, most of them new immigrants to Israel from Iraq, North Africa, and Romania.

Through the 1960s and early 1970s, Beersheva was made up of many temporary housing neighborhoods for new immigrants, called *ma'abarot*. The families in these neighborhoods had very little money, and many lived in poverty. It wasn't unusual for these families to wait five years to get a telephone in their home, or own a car. During this time, the economic situation in all of Israel was poor, and in Beersheva, jobs were exceptionally difficult to find. Ilan's parents were fortunate that they were able to find work and could afford a nice home for their two sons.

Ilan's family lived in a three-story apartment building with a large, undeveloped area behind it that had once been used as a railway station when the Turks ruled Palestine in the early 1900s. Ilan, Gadi, and their friends often played in the wide-open space behind their apartment building.

Ilan and Gadi attended Be'ery Elementary School, which was set up in an abandoned Turkish building across the street from his *shikun*. While Ilan and Gadi went to school, Eliezer worked as a technician and Tonia taught piano at the town's music conservatory. Tonia was a wonderful piano player—she had learned to play as a young girl in Poland. She taught Ilan how to play, too, and Ilan studied piano for many years as a child.

Ilan was a bright boy whom his cousin from New Jersey, Yael Sucher, described as "a ray of sunshine from the day he was born." Yael was actually Eliezer's cousin from Berlin, who had lived with the Wolfermann family in their Tel Aviv apartment after her immigration to Palestine in 1939. Yael later moved to the United States, but she remembers both Ilan and Gadi as loving, happy children. Even at a very young age, Ilan's friends and family noticed his unique qualities and personality. "In addition to his good looks and captivating smile," Yael said, "he was both kind and charming."

Many people are surprised to learn that Ilan never dreamed of becoming an astronaut when he was a boy. Ilan explained that for a young child growing up in Israel in the 1950s and 1960s, becoming an astronaut was not an option. At that time, Israel didn't have its own space program, like NASA in the United States. (Israel still doesn't have its own manned space program, but does maintain a growing satellite program and an Israel Space Agency.) Ilan did, however, have dreams of flying when he was young. He looked up to the heroic fighter pilots in the Israeli army who were so bravely defending his country and had hopes of someday becoming one of them.

Ilan also shared one popular ambition with young boys from all over the world—the dream of becoming a professional basketball star. Unfortunately, due to his small stature, he knew that playing for the Maccabi Tel Aviv (one of Israel's best professional basketball teams) was unlikely. His short height did eventually work in his favor, however, when he later became an astronaut. Since *Columbia's* shuttle cabin was only 18 square feet, he once jokingly told reporters that he would finally benefit from being short!

Ilan entered high school in September, 1968, and attended Makif Gimel High School, a gray concrete building with 400 students, divided into 10 classes per grade. In high school, Ilan *did* get the chance to play basketball and realize his "hoop dreams," when he made the high school basketball team in the 10th grade.

In high school, Ilan developed many other interests, including a passion for science. He specialized in the exact sciences—math, physics, and chemistry—and was an excellent student. Described by many of his former classmates as "smart, popular," and a "nice person and great friend," Ilan was also recalled by some of his female classmates as being the best-looking boy in school. In an interview after Ilan's death, a childhood friend remarked that "everyone knew he would go far."

Throughout high school, Ilan spent a great deal of time with his many friends playing sports, going to parties, and celebrating holidays. As is the custom in Israel, on Yom ha-Atzmaut (Israeli Independence Day) Ilan and his friends would always have a huge party, complete with a *kumzitz* (campfire).

Ilan's close friend and classmate, Reuven Segev, who is now an engineering professor at Ben Gurion University in Beersheva, remembers that Ilan received excellent grades in high school, particularly in physics and math, which were considered the most difficult subjects. Ilan was quite serious about his studies, Segev remembers, and while other boys in his class would sometimes be noisy in class, forget their homework, or joke around a lot, Ilan was the opposite. "He was very self-confident and did not need to impress anyone." According to another classmate, "He stood out without being a show-off."

When Ilan was 16, he had begun to develop the hobbies and interests that would eventually lead him toward a career in the Air Force. Motor scooters were very popular when Ilan was in 11th grade, and many of his friends bought used scooters and fixed them up for riding and racing. Ilan's scooter was blue with a custom handlebar, like a 1960s Harley Davidson motorcycle. His friends remember that Ilan's scooter was the most impressive of the bunch: immaculate and very well taken care of. They remember that he enjoyed driving his scooter very fast, and was an excellent, safe driver.

Another of Ilan's hobbies was flying. In fact, he had his first experience flying when a neighbor who worked with his father took him for a ride in his small Cessna airplane and allowed him to take over the controls. Ilan fondly remembered this event and later claimed that it was the moment he knew for sure he wanted to become a pilot and fly jets. "To this day," he said, in an interview before the shuttle launch, "[that neighbor] thinks I owe him my career!"

Ilan shared his passion for flying with his father, Eliezer. Throughout their lives, Ilan and his father remained very close, many times "gliding" together, a sport they both enjoyed immensely. Gliding is similar to flying, but performed in a glider plane, an unpowered aircraft that is dropped from a regular fueled airplane. The Wolfermann family also traveled together often. On one

11

trip, Ilan's entire family traveled to Berlin to visit the city and home where Eliezer grew up.

In addition to his regular studies, Ilan also participated in his high school Gadna program, a pre-military training program for all Israeli high school students. Ilan and his friends enjoyed Gadna because it meant not having to attend "regular" classes for a few days, or receive any homework! The Gadna program prepares Israeli high school students for service in the Israeli Army, which is mandatory for every teenager directly upon graduation from high school. Here in the United States, "scouting" is the closest thing to what Gadna training is in Israel. The big difference is that here scouting is a hobby and is voluntary, while in Israel, every boy and girl *must* attend Gadna.

Once a month in Gadna, Ilan and his classmates participated in a full-day activity such as hiking or swimming. In 10th grade, they went on a 10-day trip to a training camp in Zriffin, close to the town of Rishon LeZion near Tel Aviv. There was also a four-day Gadna trip each year: in 10th grade they went to Eilat, the southernmost city in Israel; in 11th grade to the Golan Heights, Israel's northern mountain range; and in 12th grade, to Hermon, a mountain in northern Israel—near Lebanon—famous for, among many things, its excellent skiing conditions.

In 1972, Ilan graduated first in his class from high school. The atmosphere in the country at that time was one of excitement and euphoria—Israel just having emerged victorious from the Six Day War. The 1967 Six Day War began when Israel was attacked by Arab neighbors on three borders simultaneously. The Israelis defeated the Egyptian, Syrian, and Jordanian armies in just six days. "The Air Force was the hero of the victory," Ilan's friend Reuven Segev explained at a memorial ceremony for Ilan. "We all wanted to make it there." Ilan was no exception. With his exemplary school record, his intense passion for science, and his promising flying skills, he was a natural candidate for the Air Force.

When his military service began in September 1972, Ilan was thrilled to be among those chosen to enter pilot's training school. He was now on his way to realizing his dreams of becoming an Air Force pilot.

3

The Pilot

Because of the numerous successes of the Israeli Air Force since the country's independence in 1948, and given the exceptional knowledge and skill needed to become a pilot, many men and women in Israel aspire to be selected for the Air Force, but few actually succeed. "At that time, it was a real challenge to be a pilot," Ilan once told *Lifestyles*, an internet magazine. "And you could never be sure you'd finish, because it was really hard!" It is not surprising that Ilan Ramon's family was very proud when they learned that he had passed the rigorous test requirements for admission into pilot's training.

Many Israelis who settle in Israel from other countries often change their names to Hebrew names, in honor of their new homeland. Both Ilan and Gadi changed their last name from Wolfermann to Ramon when they entered the Israeli Air Force. Using some of the same letters found in "Wolfermann," they came up with the word *ramon*, which means pomegranate. Ilan's parents kept their name Wolfermann.

Ilan attended flight-training school as an 18-year-old recruit at Hatzerim Air Force Base outside Beersheva. At the time, Ya'acov Terner—currently the mayor of Beersheva—was the commander at the flight school. He remembers Ilan as an intelligent teenager with a good heart. "I remember him for those qualities, which he carried with him throughout his life," Terner later said at a memorial service for Ilan.

Ilan excelled in pilot school. In fact, his training was so exemplary that when war broke out on Yom Kippur in 1973, Ilan was selected to fly in combat, although he was technically still a trainee with just one year of experience. The Yom Kippur War was an especially devastating war for Israel, and despite the fact that Israel was victorious, the country suffered many losses.

Ilan flew on many successful missions during the Yom Kippur War, but one memorable training flight was particularly dangerous. While he and his instructor were flying an aircraft called the Fuga, they were in a situation that called for abandoning the aircraft. A pilot cannot eject from a Fuga jet as easily as he or she can from other fighter planes. Ilan and his instructor had to crawl through the jet's fuselage (the main body of the plane) toward the tail, while the plane was airborne, and then jump out a rear bulkhead panel with their parachutes. Ilan was injured during his jump and forced to miss his pilot's training for many months. Fortunately, he recovered completely and was able to return to flight school and graduate the following year, in 1974.

Upon graduation, Ilan immediately enlisted in Israel's Air Force. From 1974 through 1976 he participated in A-4 Basic Training and Operations, and from 1976 through 1980 in training and operations on an attack aircraft known as the Mirage-IIIC.

It was in 1980, when Ilan was twenty-six years old, that he was chosen to become part of a team that would establish the first F-16 squadron in Israel. The F-16 is an American-made fighter plane that, at that time, was about to be made available to the Israeli Air Force. Once the United States made the decision to sell the Israeli Army these advanced fighter jets, the Israelis put together a team of pilots to send to the United States to learn how to operate them. Ilan and a handful of other pilots were sent to Hill Air Force Base outside Ogden, Utah, for F-16 training.

In Utah, Ilan studied everything about the F-16 and learned how to fly the jet. Dov Cohen—an engineer who spent time in Utah with Ilan, and who is now the head of space systems at Israel Aircraft Industries (the largest manufacturer of planes in Israel)—was very impressed with Ilan: "[Fighter pilots] have to be so precise, so multi-talented, so disciplined," Cohen told a newspaper reporter in Florida. "He [Ramon] had all of those qualities." Ramon quickly became such a vital part of the IAF that he would soon be chosen for one of the Air Force's most top-secret, dangerous missions ever.

4

A Hero Pilot: The Mission That Changed History

Upon returning to Israel from Utah, Ilan had logged enough F-16 flight hours and trained so proficiently on the F-16 fighter jet, that he earned the rank of Deputy Squad Commander for an F-16 Air Force Squadron. What he would soon learn was that the Israeli Air Force had big plans for him, plans that would utilize all the flying skills he had acquired in Utah.

In September 1980, there were two countries in the Middle East—Iran and Iraq—who were at war with each other. On September 27 of that year, Iran launched a secret attack on Iraq in an attempt to damage a nuclear reactor that Iraq was building in the town of Tuwaitha, approximately 10 miles west of the country's capitol, Baghdad. The Iranian bombings ended in failure, and the nuclear reactor remained intact.

At that time, dictator Saddam Hussein was the reigning power in the large Arab country of Iraq, an enemy of the tiny State of Israel. Israel feared that if Iraq developed nuclear weapons at the reactor in Tuwaitha, Saddam

Hussein would use them on Israel, and eventually the rest of the world. As far back as 1975, the Israeli government had feared the military intentions of the Iraqi leader. By 1980, Israeli intelligence sources had collected a lot of information about the Iraqi nuclear reactor and realized that it would be large enough and powerful enough to manufacture an atom bomb. So after Iran failed in its attempt to destroy the Iraqi reactor, Israel began developing its own plans to destroy it.

After many years of studying surveillance photos and reviewing mountains of intelligence information, the Israeli Defense Force (IDF) realized that an operation to destroy the Tuwaitha reactor would be best carried out by the Israeli Air Force. Initially, the Air Force considered the possibility of striking Iraq's reactor with bombs dropped from their Skyhawk and Phantom aircrafts. However, this plan was ultimately rejected because the Skyhawk and Phantom jets needed refueling during long flights and because the Israelis would have to fly over enemy territory in order to attack Iraq. There wasn't a single country situated between Israel and Iraq that Israel could count on to allow their planes to land and refuel during this sort of mission. All the countries located between Israel and Iraq were longtime enemies of the State of Israel.

For a while, the Israeli Air Force believed they would have to scratch all their plans to destroy the reactor because no assault scenario seemed possible. However, in an unexpected political development, the Shah of Iran was removed from power, and the United States decided to sell their F-16 fighter jets to Israel instead of to Iran, as originally planned. This was exactly the opportunity the Israelis were looking for. With the American F-16s, the Air

Force could execute an attack operation on the Iraqi reactor without having to refuel during the mission. The initial plan, which the Air Force had named "Operation Opera," was back on the drawing board.

Choosing pilots for such a top-secret, dangerous mission was difficult, and only the most skilled and experienced pilots could be selected. In an interview with *Israel Air Force* magazine, Brigadier General Amos Yadlin, Second Deputy Squadron Commander of the "First Jet" squadron for Operation Opera, and one of the pilots chosen for the operation, said: "It was clear to all of us that this was a very special selection for a very specific assignment." (General Yadlin later went on to become Israel's Air Force Chief of Air Staff.)

Fresh from extensive F-16 training, and a newly ranked Deputy Squad Commander, Ilan was a natural choice for participation in Operation Opera. His squadron, the "Northern Knights," was chosen to be one of two squadrons involved in the secret mission. Commander Yadlin's squadron, the "First Jet" squadron, was the other. "The only thing we were told," Commander Yadlin later explained, "was that we would have to acquire complete operational mastery of the F-16 by October."

Together, both squadrons began preparing for a dangerous mission—of which the target was a mystery. Each pilot was told that in time they would be given more details about the operation. They prepared anyway, mostly practicing air-to-air and long-distance attacks. Commander Yadlin later said he had guessed the nature of the mission by doing a little intelligence-investigating of his own. When he was asked by the mission's Operations Unit if he thought the F-16 could achieve a flying range of 600 miles, he found a ruler and a map and measured 600 miles from the Ramat David Air Base in Israel. When he found that the 600-mile point on the ruler rested on Baghdad, Iraq, he knew the operation involved an attack on Iraq.

Under the direction of Colonel Ze'ev Raz and Brigadier-General Amir Nahumi, Ilan, Commander Yadlin and the other pilots selected began to rehearse their combat operation and scenarios of what might happen if they were detected and met with resistance by the enemy (even though they still didn't know who the enemy was). Years later Ilan admitted that he had been secretly told of the nature of the operation nearly one year before it was actually carried out and had helped to create key points of Operation Opera. He had been the soldier to select the attack route, and had also navigated and planned fuel consumption for the four-hour round trip over enemy territory.

"Logistically, he achieved what was thought impossible," Commander Yadlin later said in an interview. "Ilan was only a Captain, but we knew he was the right choice for the job. He was cool-headed, modest, sort of a humble hero. Not like most macho top-gun flyers."

The official target date was originally set for January 1981 and the pilots were told about their actual attack site. Ilan and the other pilots studied the aerial photos of the reactor and memorized the details by heart. The reactor, nicknamed by the Air Force "The 17th of Tammuz," consisted of one large reactor, "Tammuz 1," and a small research reactor, "Tammuz 2." For unknown reasons, however, after all the participants in the operation had gathered at the Etzion Air Base in the Sinai Desert, the mission had to be postponed until May 7, and was then delayed again until June of that year.

Finally, on June 4, during the Shavuot holiday, while some of the pilots were at home with their families, all eight pilots received orders to return to the base. Operation Opera was back on again. Three days later, on the afternoon of June 7, eight American F-16 jets piloted by eight Israeli Air Force pilots took off, headed for Iraq.

Of the eight pilots involved in the operation, Ilan was the youngest, and was placed as the eighth pilot in formation on the mission—the last plane en route toward the reactor. This flying position was considered the most dangerous. In an interview after the mission, Ilan explained why this position was so hazardous: "For the enemy, the first jet is a surprise, the second gets his attention, by the time the third arrives, he's used to it. Usually it's the last one they manage to shoot down."

While it may seem that no one would ever want to fly last in a mission of this nature, Ilan actually volunteered for it. He felt that as the youngest pilot—and the only one unmarried and without children—he should be in that last flying formation position. Despite its dangers, Ilan was confident the operation would be successful. In a television interview after Operation Opera was completed, Ilan explained that there had been a great deal of discussion among the participants about which positions the pilots would take in the formation, and that everyone in the squadron wanted to participate: "We were all afraid we *wouldn't* be picked, that we'd be left on the ground. In the end, I was lucky."

The formation of F-16s passed over southern Jordan, then continued over the Saudi desert. Once over Iraq, the jets released their detachable fuel tanks without difficulty. Their back-up tanks were in place to fuel the remainder of the operation. After two hours, they reached the last marking point in their plans: a large lake approximately 30 miles west of Baghdad. Moments later, their target came into view: the reactor, encircled in a wall of ash and flanked with anti-aircraft balloons. Ilan and the other pilots were prepared for it all.

"The moment of attack itself is a very professional one," Commander Yadlin told *Israel Air Force* magazine. "You know the purpose well. You have rehearsed it dozens or hundreds of times. But you still have to worry about the angle, altitude and correct aiming. You have to have nerves of steel."

One by one, the pilots released their bombs over the target. Then they performed sharp turns in order to duck any missiles that might be aimed at their planes. The attack caught the Iraqis by surprise, but the pilots still had no way of knowing if they'd been detected by enemy radar. They had to be prepared for anything and everything that might happen. By the time the last two planes dropped their ammunition and prepared to leave, they were met by some resistance: a shoulder-launched missile was fired at them by Iraqis on the ground. Luckily, the missile missed.

On the trip home, the pilots began to realize that their mission had been a success. After receiving reports that the bombs from the last two planes—one of them Ilan's F-16—had destroyed the reactor, they began celebrating. "We felt wonderful," Commander Yadlin said. "Firstly, we had accomplished the mission, and secondly, the entire octet had come through."

In understanding the historic implications of the mission, and knowing that Saddam Hussein may have ultimately fired nuclear warheads at Israel had he been able to manufacture them with plutonium from the reactor, Ilan later explained his determination to defend his country in any way possible. "Maybe the answer is that you want to give back everything you've been given," he said. Commander Yadlin later remembered something Ilan told him at the time they were preparing for the Iraqi attack: "If I can prevent a second Holocaust, I'm ready to sacrifice my life for this."

5

The Air Force Colonel

Ilan Ramon, from the time he enlisted in the Israeli Air Force until the time he died aboard the space shuttle *Columbia*, embodied the spirit and the passion of the Israel Air Force pilot. Since its independence in 1948, the State of Israel has always remained a State on guard, ready to defend herself from the enemy. Surrounded by hostile countries on all sides, the Israeli Air Force is never at rest. While the State and its citizens go on with their lives, Army and Air Force soldiers in Israel remain poised at all times to defend their country.

Living in a defensive mode has unfortunately always been a way of life for Israelis, and in 1981 it was no different. Months after the daring attack on the Iraqi reactor, tension along Israel's northern border with Lebanon intensified as terrorist attacks in Israel and abroad were stepped up. Terrorist organizations based in Lebanon continually fired Katyusha rockets at Israeli settlements in the north. A cease-fire that had been declared in July 1981 was broken soon after its inception, and terrorists continued to fire at Israel's northern settlements. Throughout the year, the threat to these settlements became unbearable.

On June 3, 1982, terrorists shot Shlomo Argov, Israel's ambassador to Britain. For the Israelis, this was the final straw. Three days later, on June 6, the Israel Defense Force launched Operation "Peace for the Galilee," also known as the Lebanon War. Their intention was to rid northern Israel—the Galilee—of the constant threat from terrorists on the other side of this northern border, in the country of Lebanon. On June 9, Israeli Air Force planes, aided by ground artillery, attacked the Syrian missile array in Lebanon's Beka'a Valley. The missiles were destroyed in a matter of hours, and 29 Syrian MiG planes were shot down in the large air battle that accompanied the attack. The IAF achieved complete dominance over the Syrian Air Force, which lost 99 planes during the course of that war.

According to Israeli Air Force General David Ivri, Ilan Ramon was one of the pilots who downed 82 of the Syrian MiGs in just 46 hours of aerial combat over Lebanon. For this, Ilan was awarded the second medal of honor in his Air Force career (the first was for his role in the attack on the Iraqi reactor).

In 1983, Ilan took a break from the Air Force in order to study electronics and computer engineering at Tel Aviv University. He was an excellent student at the university, but also made time for a social life, attending parties and traveling often. On one memorable vacation, Ilan and a friend traveled to Nepal, a small country nestled between China and India, and hiked through the Himalayas for three weeks. For Ilan, that three-week trip was one of the best times of his life. He enjoyed the opportunity to hike alone for days through beautiful territory without seeing another human being. He used this peaceful time to embrace nature and reflect on his life and the things that were important to him. He described the experience as life-changing. In 1986, while still a student at Tel Aviv University, Ilan met Rona Bar Simantov at a neighbor's party. Like Ilan, Rona was a sabra, a person born and bred in the Land of Israel. Rona was a few years younger than Ilan and a student at the Wingate Institute of Physical Education and Sports, not far from Tel Aviv, where she studied reflexology. After six months of dating, Ilan and Rona were married.

In 1987, Ilan received his undergraduate degree, a Bachelor of Science degree in electronics and computer engineering. At this point he could have interviewed for a job as a scientist or teacher, but he knew his heart still belonged to the Israeli Air Force. Shortly after graduating, he decided to re-enlist in the Air Force. He later told a United Press reporter that he couldn't think of a better career for himself than in the military, especially because of his interest and training in high-tech weapons.

"I'd decided to go back to the Air Force," Ilan told *Lifestyles*, mainly because of the people that you work with there . . . They're really the best-devoted, friendly, and educated. I think the surroundings that you work in are very important and I decided I'd be better off in the Air Force where there were challenges that excite me."

Once re-enlisted, Ilan served as Deputy Squadron Commander A in the F-4 Phantom Squadron. The Phantom aircraft, nicknamed *Kurnas* (Sledgehammer) in Israel, is an American-made fighter plane that had gained notoriety in the 1973 Yom Kippur War. Ilan soon became a Phantom "ace," as skilled and knowledgeable as he'd been as an F-16 aircraft pilot in 1980.

Ilan's college degree paid off in the Air Force. In addition to his responsibilities as a Deputy Squadron Commander, Ilan worked with Israel Aircraft Industries as part of a team put together to develop an Israeli-made jet fighter plane. Ilan was instrumental in developing the *Lavi* (Lion) fighter jet, which, although it never actually became operational, was nonetheless regarded as the first military plane planned and manufactured in Israel from scratch.

For the next ten years, Ilan worked his way up through the chain of command in the IAF and became an F-16 squadron commander, head of the aircraft branch of the operations department. It was also during this time that he and Rona started their family. Their first son, Assaf, was born in 1988; their second son, Tal, was born in 1990; and their third son, Yiftach, was born in 1993. Their only daughter, Noa, was born in 1999. In 1994, Ilan received a promotion to the rank of Colonel and was assigned as Head of the Operations Department for Weapon Development and Acquisition. "I was in charge of the weapon systems for the entire Air Force," Ilan told *Lifestyles*. His job was to prioritize what needed to be developed and what needed to be purchased—everything from airplanes and weapon systems to computers and radar.

A few years later, in 1997, Ilan began to contemplate his retirement from the Air Force. Then one evening, as he sat at his desk in Israeli Air Force headquarters, he received an amazing telephone call that would drastically change his plans.

6

A Sabra in Space

The phone call that changed Ilan Ramon's career plans came nearly one year after the five-year-old son of a Jewish diplomat visited the National Air and Space Museum in Washington, D.C., with his father and asked why there had never been an Israeli astronaut.

Jeremy Issacharoff, the former political counselor at the Israeli Embassy in Washington took his son to visit that famous museum one day, and, while the two were at the space shuttle exhibit, five-year-old Dean turned to his father and asked, "Daddy, why isn't there an Israeli astronaut?"

Part of Dean's father's job at that time had been to come up with ideas to present at an upcoming summit meeting between President Clinton and Israeli Prime Minister Shimon Peres. A summit between the two leaders was being held to discuss ways in which they might establish better relations between the United States and Israel and achieve peace between Israel and her Arab enemies. Issacharoff began to wonder about his son's question: Why had there been astronauts from many other nations on NASA shuttle missions, including astronauts from Saudi Arabia, but never an astronaut from Israel? He decided to present that very question to the president of the United States.

A few days before the summit, Issacharoff received a reply from Israel's ambassador to the United States saying that President Clinton had considered his question and decided there *should* be an Israeli astronaut on a future space shuttle mission. Days later, President Clinton announced to the world that plans were under way for an American space shuttle mission that would include an Israeli astronaut. Later that year, NASA and the Israel Space Agency formed an agreement that put the wheels in motion for it to happen. But first they needed to come up with a legitimate, scientific purpose for an Israeli to travel with NASA into space.

Israeli and NASA scientists eventually decided on a Tel Aviv University research proposal called the Mediterranean Israeli Dust Experiment (MEIDEX, for short), which would investigate the impact of tiny dust particles (too small to be detected by the human eye) in the atmosphere and their effect on global climate and rainfall. Using specially designed cameras aboard a space shuttle, an Israeli astronaut could monitor dust particles from the Sahara Desert and record how they are distributed across North Africa, the Mediterranean Sea, and the Atlantic Ocean. "The hardware itself," Ilan explained in a NASA interview, "is a very sophisticated camera which can take photos—TV photos—which are very, very precise photos. We call it radiometric data." They would then send the space photos back to the scientists at Tel Aviv University for them to analyze.

The MEIDEX experiment would benefit researchers not only in Israel and the Middle East, but throughout the world as well. Tel Aviv University physics professor Zev Levin was chosen to be in charge of the scientists and research team that would lead the project. Now all that was needed was an Israeli astronaut who could meet some special criteria and was willing to travel on an upcoming space shuttle mission to conduct the necessary experiments.

The Israel Space Agency received more than two dozen applications from scientists and former pilots from all over the State of Israel who were interested in the job. But in order to fly on a space shuttle, they needed an individual who had both the education and intelligence of a scientist and the experience and skill of a pilot. They turned to the one institution in Israel where they could find candidates of this nature: the Israeli Air Force. But even in the IAF, there were few pilots who could meet all these unique specifications.

As you may remember, we left Colonel Ramon at his desk in Israel Air Force headquarters, just as his telephone was about to ring. The voice on the other end was that of Israel Air Force Chief Major General Dan Halutz, who asked Ilan if he'd like to become an astronaut. At first, Ilan was sure his colleague was joking. In Israel, the English word "astronaut" is often something you might call someone who is always distracted, or has their head "in the clouds."

"C'mon," Ilan told the caller. "I don't have time for jokes now!"

But he soon learned that this was not a joke. In fact, Ilan had everything the Air Force was looking for in a prospective astronaut. He was a gifted pilot, a great leader, and a team player. He had a technical background, and had been involved in conducting experiments while he was with the Air Force. Although it had never been a dream of his to travel to space, Ilan knew that this was an experience he couldn't pass up. If he accepted the offer, it would mean that he and Rona would have to pack up their family and move from Israel to the United States for astronaut training. It would mean long, vigorous training hours and, of course, traveling into space, a trip associated with certain risks.

For Ilan, the chance to become Israel's first astronaut was a once-in-a-lifetime opportunity: "When I was selected," Ilan said in an interview with *Yediot Achranot*, a newspaper in Israel, "I was very excited. I almost *jumped* into space!" After he was chosen, he told a writer from *Being Jewish* magazine that all sorts of images ran through his head. He pictured himself seeing the earth from space and floating around like astronauts do in movies. "Of course I didn't know too much about the space program at that time because it wasn't any kind of dream for me," Ilan said. "I was on my way to retirement from the Air Force, so it [came as] a surprise."

Ilan eventually accepted the Air Force's offer, and on June 6, 1998, he and his astronaut "backup," Lieutenant Colonel Yitzhak Mayo, moved to the United States with their families and began their astronaut training at the Johnson Space Center in Houston, Texas. (Colonel Mayo was chosen as a backup astronaut in case Ilan fell ill before the flight, or could not travel into space for any reason.)

The move was a big change for the entire Ramon family, but Ilan said it was a big adventure, too. "Leaving the State of Israel to live in the United States is by itself a very special experiment," he told *Being Jewish*. "Some of [my children] did not know a word of English and we just stuck them in public school and they had to struggle their way through."

Originally, Ilan's space mission was supposed to launch in 1999. But the space mission that year didn't present the best environment for the MEIDEX experiment Ilan was working on, so his participation was postponed. In fact, it turned out that because of various delays, Ilan waited more than two and a half years for his space mission.

Even though Ilan's family came with him to the United States, he still spent long periods of time away from them, training at Spacehab in Cape Canaveral, Florida. Ilan shuttled back and forth from the Johnson Space Center in Texas to Cape Canaveral so that his family could make a home for themselves in Houston and avoid being up-rooted every time he needed to be in Florida.

The Ramon family loved living in Houston. They quickly became part of the large Jewish community there, joining Congregation Shaar Hashalom near the Johnson Space Center and making many new friends. Many of Shaar Hashalom's congregants were fellow scientists and engineers who also worked at NASA. The Ramons were used to living side by side with other military families, just as they had in Re'ut, in Israel, a town built specially for military personnel near Tel Aviv. One family friend from Houston remembered Ilan as "an easygoing, down-to-earth, fun-loving, good-natured kind of person." The rabbi from Shaar Hashalom agreed. "Ilan and his whole family were the kindest, warmest, people you ever met," he said. "If you were in services here, you would just talk to him, [and] not realize he was the Israeli astronaut." Another rabbi from the Houston area had a similar experience. "Colonel Ramon touched people in our congregation, not only because he was a Jew and an Israeli, but because he was so anxious to make his mission one that he could share with the entire Jewish world."

In Houston, the Ramon children went to school, participated in sports and clubs and traveled together as a family as much as Ilan's long training hours would allow. "Ilan loved to travel to out-of-the-way places that were quiet," a family friend remembered, "where he could enjoy being with his kids."

Ilan's children adjusted quickly to the change as well. In fact, Ilan admitted that his children's English was almost better than his own, though theirs ended up having a sort of Texas accent. His son Assaf became an honor student in his school in Houston. "His teachers don't know that he wasn't born here," Ilan told *Lifestyles*. "My boys know that I am going to fly into space, but my little girl doesn't understand it as yet. My wife is very excited for me, but she is waiting for the moment that the shuttle will touch down and the mission will be over. As for my friends, they're very happy for me, and of course my Air Force colleagues are really envious!"

Ilan's lengthy days were spent at NASA training stations in both Florida and Texas, learning about space travel in the same way American astronauts do. At the Johnson Space Center (JSC), Ilan trained with 150 other astronauts from all over the world—Europe, Russia, Canada, Japan, South America—learning how to function in a simulated anti-gravity atmosphere, training with flight instructors, and studying shuttle technology. Ilan was the only international astronaut trainee at JSC who was not connected with the International Space Station.

The International Space Station is a satellite that remains in orbit and is inhabited by different astronauts and cosmonauts doing space research for long periods of time. It was first launched in 1998 as a cooperative effort by sixteen nations (led by the United States and Russia) and is still in the process of being completed today. Since all astronauts training for human space flights go through the same training at the JSC, Ilan trained with those astronauts preparing to travel to the International Space Station.

To prepare astronauts for weightlessness, Ilan told a reporter from *BabagaNewz* magazine (a monthly classroom magazine for Jewish students in grades four through seven) that NASA has a special airplane that uses a unique flying pattern to produce 20 to 25 seconds of zero gravity. The plane—dubbed by astronauts the "Vomit Comet"—climbs to a high altitude and then drops quickly before climbing and dropping again. While it's diving, everything inside the plane is in free fall, which simulates a feeling of weightlessness. It's like the feeling you get riding a roller coaster. "It does a maneuver in the air that involves 20–25 seconds of weightlessness," explained Ilan. "It makes you feel sick!"

Along with the six astronauts he would ultimately travel with aboard *Columbia*, Ilan concentrated on training specifically for his space mission, Mission STS-107. During his preparation for the MEIDEX experiments, the main purpose of his flight into space, Ilan was often asked what he thought about performing research that would ultimately be shared with countries that were enemies of Israel. "Science is done for the humankind wherever they are," Ilan told the *Jerusalem Post* before his launch. "It's one of every scientist's obligations to share his findings. This goes for every experiment we are to do on STS-107, including MEIDEX. The Israeli scientists are working in collaboration with NASA scientists, so everything is going to be shared."

Ilan was officially classified by NASA as a "Payload Specialist" for the space shuttle mission, a category reserved for one-time astronauts heading to space for a specific experiment. But Ilan considered himself more of a "Mission Specialist," since he was involved in so many other activities and experiments on the STS-107. "If I was [just] a Payload Specialist," he said in a pre-flight interview with NASA, "[MEIDEX] would be the only thing that I would have done. But since I'm here a longer time, and I've had the opportunity to study a lot of shuttle systems, I'm part of the crew as any other Mission Specialist."

In addition to MEIDEX, Ilan also helped with the dozens of other experiments that were set to take place aboard *Columbia*. There was the SOLE experiment, which dealt with the changes of ozone in the atmosphere; the LSP experiment, which monitored the process of soot production and ecology; and the SOFBALL (Structures of Fire Balls at Low Lewis-Numbers) experiment, which monitored balls of fire and the chemical reactions that produce the fire.

Besides the many life-science and atmospheric experiments Ilan and his crew were to conduct during the space shuttle—approximately 80 different ones—the astronauts agreed to become research projects themselves during the sixteen-day mission. Like "human guinea pigs," they planned to test the effects of certain conditions in space on their own bodies. Ilan volunteered for many of these life-science research experiments, which meant he had to give blood, saliva, and urine samples during the flight and monitor his breathing and heart rate while exercising. The ARMS (European Space Agency Advanced Respiratory Monitoring System) experiment—actually a series of eight experiments—dealt with the effects of microgravity on the body. "It's a lot of breathing," Ilan explained, "while you're in rest and while you're cycling." Another was the PhAB4—a human life experiment— which involved drawing blood and collecting urine to see how the atmosphere in space affected the human body.

Aside from MEIDEX, Ilan's most eagerly anticipated space project was the series of STARS experiments (Space Technology and Research Students) he would help conduct, because they involved the participation of children from all over the world. "On STARS we have six experiments from [all over] the whole world," Ilan explained. Classrooms of students participated in STARS from China, Japan, the United States, and Israel. The Israeli students were from Yonatan Netanyahu ORT Motzkin High School in Kiryat Motzkin, north of Haifa. Ilan was to supervise their chemistry experiments while in space. Teenagers at the school developed a scientific experiment called "The Chemical Garden," which examined how crystals grow in space. For the experiment, the students chose blue cobalt crystals and white calcium crystals to represent the colors of the Israeli flag.

Other STARS experiments dealt with different research topics, such as the lifecycle of silkworms in space. "What is exciting about STARS," Ilan said in a NASA interview about the program, "is that the students are the one[s] who had the idea, planned the experiment, planned how it worked, participated in putting the hardware together, and of course [will] analyze [the results] postflight." Ilan went on to say, "I think that for kids, space is inspiring. It's a great tool to attract students to study science . . . [to] know all the crew that supports such a mission, and be [a] part of it."

It was more than two years into his training before Ilan would meet the crew with whom he was to spend sixteen days in space. Their names were Rick Husband, Willie McCool, Kalpana Chawla, Mike Anderson, Laurel Clark, and David Brown, and during the course of their training, they would become as close as any seven, unrelated people could become. Like family, the STS-107 crew would learn to live together, work together, eat together, and sleep side by side.

Official portrait of astronaut Ilan Ramon (colonel, Israel Air Force), payload specialist representing the Israeli Space Agency. (Courtesy of National Aeronautics and Space Administration [NASA])

Ilan (front row far left, leaning in) as a teenager with his friends in the halls of Makif Gimel High School in Israel. (Courtesy of Ezra Akirav)

Ilan (far right with stick in hand) and classmates on one of his Gadna trips. Gadna is a pre-military training program for all Israeli high school students that prepares them for service in the Israeli Army, required of every Israeli teenager upon graduation from high school. (Courtesy of Ezra Akirav)

Ilan Ramon (second from the left) and Professor Zev Levin (far right), head of the MEIDEX (Mediterranean Israeli Dust Experiment) research project, meet with three science students at Tel Aviv University. The experiment, which Ilan worked on while he was in orbit, investigated the impact of tiny dust particles in the atmosphere and their effect on global climate and rainfall. (Courtesy of Michal Roche-Ben Ami, Tel Aviv University)

Ilan with Professor Itmar Rabinovich, president of Tel Aviv University, during a visit in May, 2000. (Courtesy of Michal Roche-Ben Ami, Tel Aviv University)

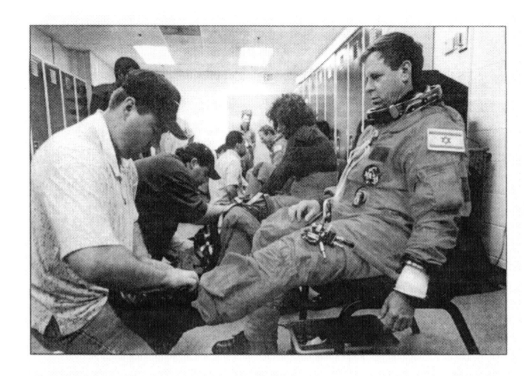

Ilan takes a break during the STS-107 crew's 50-mile hike through Wyoming's Rocky Mountains as part of the National Outdoor Leadership School's (NOLS) Professional Training Institute expedition in August, 2001. Ilan was said to make the best coffee during the back-packing trip, which he jokingly called "cowboy" coffee. (Courtesy of NOLS)

Ilan makes his way through a river during the crew's NOLS expedition through the Rocky Mountains. For 11 days they were completely cut off from the outside world as they helped one another cope with the hardships of the difficult terrain. The astronauts journeyed into the wilderness as a NASA crew, but came back as a family. (Courtesy of NOLS)

Official STS-107 insignia. The mission conducted microgravity and earth science investigations during its 16 days in orbit. The central element of the patch is the microgravity symbol flowing into rays of the astronaut symbol. The constellation Columbia *(the dove) was chosen to symbolize peace on Earth and the space shuttle* Columbia. *The seven stars (on the left wing) represent the mission crew members, and their names appear along the perimeter of the insignia. The Israeli flag adjacent to Ilan's name (on the right wing) is to honor him as the first Israeli to fly on the space shuttle. (Courtesy of NASA)*

Ilan (third from the right) and other members of the STS-107 crew, as they roughed it during their NOLS Professional Training Institute expedition. They were responsible for carrying their own supplies and tents as they hiked for six miles through the Rocky Mountains in Wyoming. The trip was a test of each member's endurance and helped to determine how well they could work together as a team. (Courtesy of NOLS)

Columbia, *after rollback of the Rotating Service Structure on Launch Pad 9A. Visible are two of the three access arms that provided services or access to the shuttle while it was waiting to be launched. (Courtesy of NASA)*

Ilan Ramon as he arrived at the Kennedy Space Center in Florida to take part in the Terminal Countdown Demonstration activities, which included a simulated launch countdown. (Courtesy of NASA)

Ilan in orbit aboard Columbia *with the Chemical Garden, the Israeli-sponsored experiment that was part of the Space Technology and Research Students (STARS) payload flown in the SPACEHAB Research Double Module. (Courtesy of NASA)*

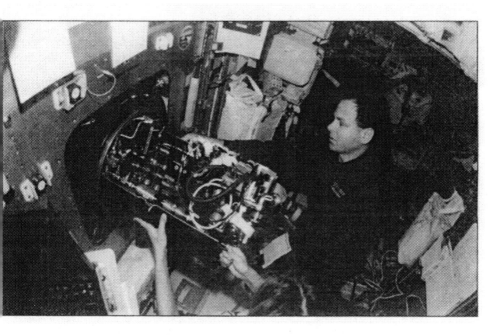

Ilan and astronaut Kalpana Chawla (bottom, partially out of picture) as they work with the Combustion Module-2 (CM-2) facility in the SPACEHAB Research Double Module aboard Columbia. *(Courtesy of NASA)*

Ilan in the SPACEHAB, working with the STARS experiment. The STARS payload included the following: The Chemical Garden, sponsored by Israel; Spiders in Space (Astrospiders), sponsored by Australia; Silkworm Lifecycle During Space Flight, sponsored by China; Flight of the Medaka Fish, sponsored by Japan; Carpenter Bees in Space, sponsored by Liechtenstein; and Ant Colony, sponsored by the United States. (Courtesy of NASA)

Astronaut David M. Brown (bottom), mission specialist, exercises on the Bicycle Ergometer as Ilan (floating above) types on a laptop computer on the aft deck aboard Columbia. *(Courtesy of NASA)*

Rona Ramon, Ilan's widow, and Eliezer Wolfermann, Ilan's father, (left) receiving an award in May, 2003, from Professor Itmar Rabinovich (right), president of Tel Aviv University, on behalf of Ilan's contribution to science. (Courtesy of Michal Roche-Ben Ami, Tel Aviv University)

The seven STS-107 crewmembers. Seated in front: Rick D. Husband (left), mission commander, and William C. McCool (right), pilot. Standing are (from left to right) astronauts David M. Brown, Laurel B. Clark, Kalpana Chawla, and Michael P. Anderson, all mission specialists, and Ilan Ramon, payload specialist, representing the Israeli Space Agency. (Courtesy of NASA)

The actual launch of Columbia *on mission STS-107, as it is reflected in nearby water at Kennedy Space Center, Florida. Liftoff occurred at 10:30 A.M. EST on January 16, 2003.*
(Courtesy of NASA)

Artist's drawing of the Ilan Ramon Space Play Park in Beersheva, built by the Beersheva Foundation to provide the children of Israel with a place to play while learning about their fallen hero. (Courtesy of the Beersheva Foundation)

7

STS-107: Like Family

Knowing Ilan is truly a privilege. He is easily one of the best people, if not the best person, I've met and worked with. I've learned tremendously from him.

Kalpana Chawla, *Columbia* STS-107

Ilan is much more than a payload specialist. Ilan is fully integrated into every aspect of the mission; he is not an observer, he's a full member of the crew in every way.

Commander Rick Husband, *Columbia* STS-107

Ramon [is] a wonderful individual . . . . He's a true pleasure to have around. He's a hard charger— wonderfully warm and personable. We've come to embrace and love Ilan.

Willie McCool, *Columbia* STS-107

Ilan's a great guy—he's very calm, very cool. He's hard to upset; he's got a very calm nature about him. Very confident, easy going.

Mike Anderson, *Columbia* STS-107

These guys were a team for life.

Andrew Cline, STS-107 Training Instructor

Because of repeated delays in getting their space shuttle mission off the ground, the crew had more time than those on previous missions to get to know one another before lifting off. They knew one another's families, shared baby-sitters, birthdays, recipes, and heartaches. Together they were put through extreme training and testing trips by NASA—once in a five-day outdoor trek in Canada's freezing weather, and once in a raft adrift in Russian waters. But it was the eleven days they spent in the mountains of Wyoming that truly bonded these seven individuals from all different walks of life. The astronauts journeyed into the wilderness as a NASA crew, but they came back as a family.

Shortly after Ilan began training with his American crew mates for the space shuttle mission, NASA decided that the seven astronauts could benefit from a little "to-getherness," and togetherness it was as they embarked on an expedition through the Rocky Mountains in Wyoming. They spent 24 hours a day together, cut off completely from the rest of the world. This was primarily a journey of endurance: a grueling week and a half of tramping through the Wyoming wilderness with just the backpacks on their backs and enough food for the hike. But the trip was more than just a test of each crew member's endurance, it was also to determine leadership skills and how well they could work together as a team.

The leadership program at NASA is aimed at building problem-solving skills, stimulating healthy group dynamics, and teaching individuals to manage stress. NASA trains all its astronauts this way in an effort to prepare them for some of the obstacles they may face living in such close quarters during a space mission. This difficult expedition was ultimately a huge success for the STS-107 crew: their adventures scaling the Rocky Mountains and sleeping under the stars, head to head, turned them into one of the closest crews in NASA's history.

Their journey began in August 2001, as the seven astronauts left Houston and headed for the small town of Lander, Wyoming, where the National Outdoor Leadership School was located. In Lander, they were joined by two training instructors, Andrew Cline and John Kanengieter, and then set off by foot into a remote mountain range. "Upon arrival, we were briefed on what we could expect in the next two weeks," Ilan wrote in a series of articles called "From an Astronaut's Diary" for *Israel Air Force* magazine. "We received backpacks, sleeping bags, cooking utensils, and food to last the entire expedition." They were all responsible for carrying their own supplies and tents.

Ilan and his six crewmates roughed it in the mountains, hiking for six miles a day and learning to adapt to the thin mountain air. Each day a different pair would be chosen as "leaders" of the group, responsible for supervising hikes and solving problems. "They decided on the day's order, direction and navigation," Ilan wrote about the "leaders." "At the end of the day we were instructed on various topics—how to set up a tent, how to store food in bear country, what to do if you find a bear in the vicinity, how to cook meals, how to brush your teeth, and [how to] make 'nature call' without leaving a trace.

"The hiking itself varied daily," Ilan wrote. "There were days with a more level terrain and there were days where we climbed over tall mountains. The terrain was stunning in its beauty. Huge mountain ranges were all around, and beautiful Alpine lakes [were situated] between them. Despite the freezing temperature of the water, we, of course, bathed in them."

The mountains were high, with altitudes ranging between 10,000 and 13,000 feet, and climbing them with 66-pound backpacks strapped to their backs wasn't easy! "But that's the whole point," Ilan wrote. "To challenge yourself, to bring yourself to a stressful situation, to see how you handle yourself personally and as part of a team."

There was also some time for relaxation, and the crew was able to go fishing and swim every day. They especially enjoyed bird-watching and discovering different varieties of flora and fauna, often joking that they would have been great contestants on the TV show *Survivor*. At night they would all lie under the stars and point out passing satellites. "They knew what kind each was," trainer Andrew told *People* magazine, "based on how fast and [their] direction. It was just so cool listening to them." When they weren't star-gazing at night, the astronauts slept in three tents: the Red Team (Ilan, Rick, Laurel, and Kalpana) sharing one tent; the Blue Team (Dave, Willie, and Mike) sharing another; and the training instructors in the third.

The highlight of the expedition was the group's climb to the top of the Wind River Peak, the tallest mountain in the region at 13,192 feet. Before beginning their climb, according to trainer John, they had a lengthy discussion about how they would proceed: Should they all go up together as one team or split up and leave one team back at camp? Eventually they decided that being one team meant they would all go up together.

The crew set out at 5 A.M. and reached the summit of the mountain just after 11:00 A.M. "The climb was difficult and exhausting," Ilan wrote. "There were areas with boulders that you had to skip over and patches of snow [that were even] higher. The view was breathtaking." At the peak they held up a NASA patch and then posed for photographs. They all laughed when one of the instructors pulled out a cell phone that he'd been secretly hiding during the trip and called NASA headquarters in Houston. "*Columbia* has landed!" they all chimed into the phone.

"We got to learn a lot about how each of us, as individuals, deals with situations," Rick Husband said after the trip in an interview with the Jewish Telegraph Agency. "You learn to work together, to pull together, and . . . when you come back you know each other's strengths and weaknesses.

"In the course of the expedition," Ilan wrote, "we went through days of hard physical work, we took care of buddies experiencing height sickness, [we] helped each other by sharing the backpack load, [we] relieved teammates who developed knee injuries, and [we] coped with a few decisions we had to make as a team. We were cut off completely by the outside world. When all's said and done, despite the difficulty, it was a great experience for everyone. The contribution these two weeks made to the team is immense. Today we know each other much more deeply, and there's no doubt that this will play a role in our performance in the space mission."

Ilan's words best summed up how members of the STS-107 crew felt about one another. In the months following their Rocky Mountain expedition, they went almost everywhere together, proud of their upcoming space mission, and proud to represent NASA. They traveled with an STS-107 mascot—a little toy hamster that sang "Kung Fu Fighting." At the NASA holiday party a month before the launch, they danced around together in paper crowns and sported temporary "STS-107" tattoos, and wherever they went, it was always as a group.

Ilan held his fellow crew mates in such high regard that, according to a *Jerusalem Post* article, he even sent NASA an e-mail from orbit asking them to make sure to reassign all seven astronauts immediately after the mission, so that they could all remain together on future missions. He said he couldn't imagine being part of, or flying with, a crew that was more deserving, talented, or capable.

8

Preparing for Space

We are going into space to perform research for everybody in the world, for better health, better education, for getting the kids of the world excited about space and about science.

Ilan Ramon, *The Miami Herald*

Though the launch date for *Columbia*'s STS-107 space mission had been postponed various times, it became apparent that the next scheduled launch date in early 2003 was going to be a "go." Ilan and the other six astronauts began to think about the personal items they wanted to bring with them into space. With limited room on the shuttle, NASA permitted the crew ten personal items each.

In addition to the personal items Ilan chose to bring with him, he also selected some very symbolic items. He searched for things he felt would represent the entire Jewish people—their history, their country, and their culture. Ilan felt it was his responsibility to make this space journey not only about research and personal experience, but about bringing to light the rich heritage of the Jewish people and the citizens of Israel.

Among the personal items Ilan took with him were items given to him by his family: a necklace from his wife; a watch from his father; and photos and letters from his children and his brother, Gadi. Ilan stowed these items under *Columbia's* floor in the space permitted by NASA for additional storage. The personal items Ilan received from his family were important—especially when he was feeling "homesick"—but it was the many symbolic Judaic artifacts Ilan took with him that would ultimately catch the attention of the world. Knowing this, he considered his choices carefully.

His first wish was to find an object of importance that had survived the Holocaust. This object, he knew, would become a symbol of what happened to the Jewish people during the darkest time in their history. He wanted to bring something he could hold up during a video conference while in orbit, something he could tell the world about, to help them understand the atrocities that fell upon the Jewish people during World War II. "I decided to take something with me into space that would symbolize the Holocaust survivors," Ilan told *BabagaNewz* magazine before the flight, "and those who did not survive."

The first object Ilan found was a miniature Torah—only four inches tall—that had been used by a fellow scientist during the time he was imprisoned in Bergen-Belsen, a concentration camp in Germany. Ilan later told the story of this tiny Torah as he spoke to the world on January 21, 2003, while he was in orbit.

"This was given by a rabbi to a scared, thin young boy in Bergen-Belsen," Ilan said, speaking softly, via satellite from space. He held the little Torah up for the camera that was transmitting video footage back to Earth. "It repre-

48

sents more than anything the ability of the Jewish people to survive. From horrible periods, black days, to reach periods of hope and belief in the future."

Ilan first noticed the Torah on a shelf at the home of a colleague named Yehoyachin Yosef, with whom Ilan had been working on the MEIDEX experiment for the shuttle mission. When he'd asked Yehoyachin about the Torah, Yehoyachin told Ilan it was the Torah he'd read from during a secret Bar Mitzvah ceremony in Bergen-Belsen in 1944. The scientist went on to tell Ilan the whole history of the miniature Torah:

When Yehoyachin was approaching his thirteenth birthday in the camp, he began studying for his Bar Mitzvah. A rabbi, who was also a prisoner at the camp, taught him to read from the Torah in secret every night. The Torah had been made so small so that it could be easily hidden inside a mattress, or behind the wall of the prison barracks. At the time, any objects of a Jewish nature were strictly forbidden by the Nazis. In fact, if it had been found, Yehoyachin and the rabbi would surely have been put to death.

Yehoyachin went on to recall his short Bar Mitzvah ceremony, which took place in the prison barracks before dawn, by candlelight. "There were people listening in the beds all around," Yehoyachin—now 71 years old—told the *Washington Post* in an interview. It was the same story he had told to Ilan that day at his home in Tel Aviv.

"Afterwards, everybody congratulated me. Somebody fished out a piece of chocolate that he had been saving, and somebody else brought out a tiny deck of playing cards. Everybody told me, 'You are a Bar Mitzvah boy now. You are an adult now.' And I was very happy."

After the ceremony, the rabbi presented Yehoyachin with a special gift: the Torah to keep. "This little Sefer Torah is yours to keep now," he'd told Yehoyachin, "because I'm sure that I will not get out of here alive. And you maybe will." Yehoyachin accepted the precious gift, on the condition that should he ever be liberated from the camp, he would retell the story of the Torah and the horrors that the Jews faced at Bergen-Belsen.

Yehoyachin and his family were a few of the lucky survivors liberated from Bergen-Belsen in 1945. His family managed to obtain fake passports and sail on a British military ship to Israel, where they ultimately received citizenship. Yehoyachin and his family now live in Tel Aviv.

When Ilan heard the incredible story of Yehoyachin and the miniature Torah, he knew the Torah would make an appropriate addition to the space mission. Weeks after seeing the Torah for the first time, Ilan called Yehoyachin and asked permission to bring the Torah into space. Yehoyachin agreed on the same condition that had been presented to him by the rabbi in 1944—that the story of the Torah and the horror the Jews faced during the Holocaust would be told. In an emotional news conference between Ilan and Israeli Prime Minister Ariel Sharon held on January 21, 2003, during the space mission, Ilan held up the Torah and recalled the Holocaust and Yehoyachin's story. He also mentioned the 18 months his own mother had spent in Auschwitz during the Holocaust. "I am moved to hold this," he said.

In truth, the miniature Torah was not the first Torah ever to travel into space. In 1996, astronaut Jeffery Hoffman, also aboard the *Columbia*, read from the Torah over Israel on *Shabbat*, according the Houston rabbi of the temple Hoffman belongs to. "It was very dramatic," the rabbi said in an interview with *Forward*. He also added that the Torah is now known by the congregation as the "Space Torah" and is used by the children who become a Bar or Bat Mitzvah.

Ilan felt compelled to bring a second Holocaust artifact with him into space. This item was a pen-and-ink drawing entitled "Moon Landscape," created by a Jewish boy from Prague, Czechoslovakia, named Petr Ginz. Ilan discovered the drawing at Yad Vashem, the Holocaust Museum in Israel, and asked the museum director if he could obtain a copy of the drawing to bring with him on the shuttle.

Petr Ginz was a 14-year-old prisoner at the Czechoslovakian concentration camp Theresienstadt. He was later deported to Auschwitz where, at age 16, he was killed by the Nazis. While incarcerated in Theresienstadt along with 92 other teenage boys in a cell block called "Home One," Petr created a secret magazine called *Vedem (Vanguard)*. *Vedem* featured poems, drawings, stories, interviews and humorous pieces about life in the camp, all written by the boys. Though it's hard to believe anyone could find humor in their situation, the teenagers knew creating funny, entertaining stories would provide at least some happiness to the young prisoners. Every Friday night, in darkness, the boys read each other their stories and articles in an effort to keep their spirits up in the dismal cell.

By the end of World War II, all but one of the boys had been deported to Auschwitz. Only 15 of them survived after that. Petr did not survive, but *Vedem* did. It was hidden in Home One, then retrieved when World War II was over. Many of Petr's drawings were recovered and are now kept at Yad Vashem. "Moon Landscape," the drawing chosen by Ilan, depicts Petr's vision of what the Earth looked like as seen from the moon. Ilan was captivated after seeing the drawing for the first time. He knew he'd found another appropriate artifact to bring on the mission. "I feel that my journey fulfills the dream of Petr Ginz, 58 years later," he said in a public statement before boarding the shuttle.

In addition to the Holocaust artifacts, Ilan also brought along other items that he felt "emphasized the unity of the people of Israel and the Jewish communities abroad."

1. A silver and copper barbed-wire mezuzah that contained tiny scrolls with inscriptions from the Book of Deuteronomy that was hand-crafted by the granddaughter of a Holocaust survivor.

2. A silver *Kiddush Cup* that Ilan eventually used to mark *Shabbat*—along with his fellow crew mates—in space.

3. A menorah and a pocket-size version of the Bible on microfiche film, given to him by the president of Israel, Moshe Katzav.

4. A copy of the Book of Psalms.

5. The banner of the president of Israel.

6. The logo of Tel Aviv University, where Ilan had studied and where the MEIDEX scientists were from.

7. Music from Arik Einstein, a popular Israeli singer.

8. A copy of *Tefillat Haderech*, the Jewish traveler's prayer for a safe journey.

9. A dollar bill autographed by the late Lubavitcher Rebbe Menachem Schneersohn, given to Ilan by a

rabbi from the Satellite Beach Chabad Jewish Community Center.

10. A handful of soil from *Eretz Yisra'el*, an Israeli flag which he hung proudly in the cabin, and a coin minted in Jerusalem in the year 69 C.E.

By his own admission, Ilan was a secular Jew. He occasionally attended services at his temple in Houston, and though he did not observe *Shabbat* at home, he felt compelled to observe it in space. By doing so, he demonstrated a respect for the Jewish tradition and a sensitivity for the feelings of his observant fellow Israelis. "Ilan Ramon understood that being the first Israeli astronaut brought with it great responsibilities, not just to Israel, but also to Jews worldwide," Rabbi Stuart Federow, the rabbi from Ilan's Houston synagogue, wrote in an e-mail after the astronaut's death. Ilan expressed the same sentiments in all the pre-flight interviews he gave. "It's symbolic," he told the *Jerusalem Post* about his decision. "I thought it would be nice to represent all kinds of Jews, including religious ones." He joked that if the mission commander agreed, he might even affix a mezuzah to the shuttle door!

As excited as he was to observe *Shabbat* in space, Ilan met with a few problems in trying to prepare. Since "unofficially" he would not be experiencing a 24-hour day at the end of a typical seven-day week, and Jewish law dictates that the traditional day of rest occurs every seven days from sundown to sundown, Ilan figured that in space he'd have to observe *Shabbat* every ten and a half hours. With all the research work he had to do aboard the shuttle, that would be impossible. For guidance, he discussed his dilemma with two rabbis he'd met in Florida.

"I told them that we will orbit the Earth every 90 minutes and every 40 minutes it changes from day to night," Ilan said in an interview. He pointed out that following the Jewish calendar in space would also bring Rosh Hashanah (the Jewish New Year) every 20 days.

What they eventually decided, after much discussion, was that Ilan would mark *Shabbat* according to when it began and ended—on Houston time. It just wasn't feasible to follow the "sun" to keep track of the time. Ilan eventually spent three *Shabbats* in space, during one of which he recited the blessing over the wine with his crewmates, holding the *Kiddush Cup* up for the camera. That video footage was transmitted all over the world via satellite. He even figured out a way to pour wine in space: by inserting a straw into the hole of a child's sipping cup!

Rabbi Federow recalled a pre-launch event that clearly demonstrated Ilan's deep commitment to his Jewish tradition. Although it had been a secret at the time, Rabbi Federow later told a newspaper reporter how Ilan had once asked NASA to reschedule the space shuttle's launch because the date fell on a solemn Jewish holiday. According to Rabbi Federow, the launch was scheduled to take place on July 18, 2002. "Then he [Ilan] learned that July 18 fell during the Jewish holiday of Tisha be-Av. Ilan spoke to the commander of the mission," Rabbi Federow said, "and for the first time in NASA history, the launch was rescheduled for the next day, a Friday. No launch had ever been scheduled for a Friday before. No launch had ever been postponed for purely religious reasons."

Although Ilan did his best to honor the *Shabbat* while aboard *Columbia*, he was usually too busy with important experiments to adhere to its laws completely. Because Ilan's work in space was too limited and too vital for him to take a full day of "rest," he was given "permission" by the rabbis to conduct his experiments and work through Shabbat.

Perhaps the best-known example of Ilan's Jewish pride aboard *Columbia*, was his decision to keep kosher during the mission. While there have been a few Jewish astronauts in the past—like Judith Resnick, who died in the *Challenger* shuttle explosion in 1988, Jeffrey Hoffman who also flew on the *Columbia* in 1996, and David Wolf, who was aboard the space shuttle *Endeavor* in 2001—no astronaut had ever requested kosher food on a space mission.

NASA did their best to accommodate the first-ever kosher space traveler. NASA System Manager for food, Vickie Kloeris, contacted a company called My Own Meals in Deerfield, Illinois, that sells certified kosher food in "thermostabilized" sealed pouches to the military and to kosher campers. The food, which has a shelf-life of three years, is perfect for space flight and can be opened, warmed, and eaten in orbit.

Of ten kosher choices, Ilan selected five: Florentine lasagna, beef stew, chicken Mediterranean, "My Kind of Chicken" (a chicken prepared with brown rice, peas ,and carrots), and "Old World Stew" (Middle Eastern–flavored beef with brown rice, zucchini, and pinto beans). He also chose a few pasta meals prepared with garden vegetables and cheese tortellini, rather than the nonkosher alternatives popular on space missions, like shrimp cocktail. As astronauts often do in space, Ilan and his crewmates shared and traded meals. According to Ilan, the STS-107 crew thoroughly enjoyed the kosher fare.

Ilan and the STS-107 astronauts continued their training for the mission, right through 2002. In December 2002, they took part in a mission simulation to help them best prepare for what to expect during the "real thing." During the three years prior to Ilan's flight, he was asked by the Israeli Air Force to contribute a series of articles about his training to *Israel Air Force* magazine, which is no longer published. Ilan wrote his last article in the series, "From an Astronaut's Diary," in December 2002, before his last mission simulator training exercise. What follows is the article as it appeared in that magazine:

FROM AN ASTRONAUT'S DIARY

By Ilan Ramon

Hello everybody. This past week the space shuttle Endeavor blasted off into space, and now here we are again, "Prime Crew," that is to say, we are the crew that will fly the next shuttle into space! We, being the crew of space flight STS-107.

This time, it looks like everything is progressing well, and everyone is doing their best to ensure that the flight takes off on time. NASA has said that it will make sure the flight takes off on time, whatever the cost, including making people work on holidays. The only thing that could delay this flight would be security problems. This time, there is a feeling that we are making progress in the right direction. The crew's preparations, as well as the preparations of the rest of the people involved in the shuttle's journey into space (and we are talking about hundreds of people) have entered the final stages.

Next week we will be carrying out a long training exercise in the simulator. This exercise will last two full days and will simulate two flight days out of the 16 days that we will be in space. Following our two-day simulation, we have two other training exercises, also in the simulator. Both of these exercises include full simulations of situations we will have to face in space, and we will even be required to wear our space suits.

The first simulation will be the first four hours of the flight, including the nine minutes prior to lift off. In these four hours we have to transform the shuttle from rocket configuration to shuttle configuration, or in other words, to transform the shuttle into a space laboratory. This laboratory will enable us to carry out the dozens of experiments we have planned to conduct during our 16 days in space.

The second training exercise will simulate the last five hours of flight. In these last five hours we have to prepare the space shuttle for landing. Like a plane with no engine and from an altitude of 240 km [approximately 144 miles] and a speed of 28,000 km [approximately 16,600 miles] an hour (8 km/second [approximately 4.5 miles/second]) we have to land our shuttle at Florida's Cape Canaveral.

These two phases of the journey are the busiest and most critical to the flight, especially the first, which determines how the rest of the flight will progress. In our first four hours in space, Laurel and I, (Laurel is one of the three mission specialists) will open the laboratory situated in the back of the space shuttle. After opening the laboratory, we will hover into it through two openings and a pipe, and set it up for use. That is to say, we will switch on the electricity, the air pressure and communications devices, which will enable us to carry out our experiments.

The week after our two simulation exercises, we will all be flown to Cape Canaveral for the general rehearsal before the actual flight. The general rehearsal, also known as Terminal Count Down Test (TCDT), lasts for three full days. During these three days we will experience a simulation of everything we have to do in the last three days leading up to lift off. The rehearsal ends with something called "T-Zero", which is basically a rehearsal of the lift-off itself.

Aside from all the training exercises and rehearsals, we also have to study in our own time. There are hundreds, if not thousands, of things that we have to know and remember for our 16-day voyage. Sometimes I think to myself, why so many training exercises for merely 16 days in space? The answer is that the whole operation is so intricate and complicated. To get everything right and to ensure that everything is executed as planned, much time and many exercises are required.

The Real Excitement Has Not Even Started!

Ok, so we were supposed to have been in space two years ago already, but that's just the way things go and now the preparations and training are stepping up, as take-off finally nears. And this time, we all feel that it is really going to happen, even if we are not yet feeling the excitement. The experienced astronauts here at NASA tell us that the real excitement only starts a few days before the actual lift-off. I can tell you that we are all very much looking forward to that moment.

Cross your fingers for us!

9

Rocketing into the "Blue and White" Sky

I left Israel as a shaliach, a representative of Israel and the air force. After more than four years of training in the United States and dozens of meetings in Jewish communities, I feel that I am now representing the Jewish people.

Ilan Ramon, *Baltimore Jewish Times*, January 10, 2003

After four years of training, three postponements, and a whole lot of anticipation, the launch day finally arrived. On Thursday, January 16, 2003, Israeli Air Force Colonel turned astronaut, Ilan Ramon, was about to make history.

In fact, the shuttle "launch" process actually began days before for Ilan and the STS-107 crew. The official countdown for *Columbia* began late on January 12 as the astronauts entered a specially quarantined environment to prepare their bodies for living in space without oxygen. After reporting to the Kennedy Space Center at Cape Canaveral that Sunday, they remained in the simulated space environment until take-off. They had already said their good-bys to family members and friends, for they would not get the chance to see them again before lifting off.

In addition to Rona, Assaf, Tal, Yiftach, and Noa, there were many other family members and friends who had gathered in Cocoa Beach, Florida, to watch *Columbia* lift off. Ilan's father, Eliezer, had made the trip from Israel for the launch, as had Ilan's brother, Gadi. Ilan's mother, Tonia, was too ill to make the trip to the United States. (Tonia Wolfermann passed away one month after the *Columbia* tragedy.)

Each astronaut had been given ample time to spend with their family before heading into quarantine. A few days before, the astronauts threw a pre-flight party at one of the NASA installations. Each crew member was allowed to invite five guests to the party, and Ilan chose Rona, his father, his brother, Rona's brother, and Roni Shalein, a close friend from Moshav Nahalal in Israel. "For me, this was really exciting," Shalein told Israel's *Ha'Aretz* newspaper. "To come from the cow shed at Nahalal and spend time with seven astronauts on their way into space!"

At the party, Rona presented Ilan with some poetry and personal effects to take aboard the shuttle. Gadi had written a letter to his brother, but asked that it be stowed aboard *Columbia* beforehand so Ilan would not find it until he was in space. Ilan's oldest son, Assaf, also left his father a letter to be opened in orbit only.

After an emotional "good-by," Ilan entered quarantine confinement with the other astronauts. "Happy to be here," Ilan told reporters before entering quarantine. "It's been a long road for us," fellow crew member Kalpana Chawla added. The launch was four days away, but there was still a lot of preparation to be done.

While Ilan was busy gathering the tools he would need for his experiments, the other Ramons were busy as well. There were more receptions to attend, press conferences to speak at, and preparations to be made to ensure that each family member and friend would receive the proper clearance to view the shuttle launch.

On the morning before the historic launch, Ilan's entourage of well-wishers—family, friends, dignitaries, scientists, students—completely took over the Cocoa Beach IHOP (International House of Pancakes) for breakfast. There were nearly fifty family members and friends lining the restaurant booths, countertops, and tables at the pancake house, and though it was a quick trip in and out for breakfast, it was certainly a memorable one.

After their breakfast, the group was whisked off to the Kennedy Space Center for a private tour of the facility and a reception in honor of the astronauts. Israel's ambassador to the United States, Daniel Ayalon, was there, too, excited and proud of his compatriot. Other guests included Aby Hareven, the director of the Israel Space Agency, many military officials, science students, and a local 25-member delegation from the Jewish Federation of Brevard County, Florida. One rabbi from that Federation had also prearranged to have countdown coverage of the launch broadcast over the radio in Hebrew for all the Israelis who had flown in to see the launch.

Later that evening, there was a second reception—this time for 300 people—held at the Hilton hotel. Rona spoke at the podium that night, expressing her and her husband's appreciation to the governments of the United States and Israel. In the days and hours leading to lift-off, the FBI and other federal agents kept a tight watch on the Kennedy Space Center, the areas surrounding it, and on the Ramon family. To help protect Ilan, the STS-107 crew and their families from a possible terrorist attack, NASA and the U.S. military closed roads, restricted the number of civilian sightseers, and sent fighter jets, helicopter patrols, and SWAT teams to guard the entire area. Unfortunately, because of the difficult times we live in, there is always the threat of a terrorist attack at visible events such as a space shuttle launch. While no attack was expected, both the Israeli and the American law enforcement officials wanted to be prepared.

Ilan had no concerns over security, placing his trust completely in the hands of the local and government law enforcement in Florida. "NASA security and Brevard County security were unbelievable and helpful," Ilan told CNN while in orbit. "I didn't have any doubt that everything would go really [well], and so it did."

In the early morning hours of January 13, countdown for *Columbia* officially began. There were a number of factors, however, that could jeopardize liftoff. Weather conditions in the area, for example, were a large concern for NASA. Unfavorable weather—even seconds before a launch—could result in an aborted take-off. But on January 13, weather reports for that Thursday were being predicted as "very favorable." The actual target launch time would be determined on January 15, the day before lift-off.

While Ilan and his crewmates spent time in quarantine, NASA engineers at the Space Center prepared the shuttle for launch. Engineers and inspectors tested everything in the shuttle—from the fuel tanks right down to the shuttle toilet! All the gear the crew needed for the mission, as well as several experiments, were stowed in the spacecraft cabin, along with a few living creatures—like rats and silkworms—that were part of the experiments themselves. On the morning of January 14, two days before lift-off, *Columbia's* launch countdown was proceeding smoothly. There was a minor weather concern as clouds were spotted coming off the ocean, but it had little chance of affecting the lift-off.

Everybody was busy. The shuttle test director serviced the on-board cryogenic fuel storage tanks and performed an engine system check that afternoon. In addition, the Spacehab research double module—a separate section of the shuttle that carried many of *Columbia's* experiments—was powered up while some last-minute loading took place. The entire loading process would take approximately 20 hours to complete.

The following day, January 15, the day before lift-off, a launch time for *Columbia* was officially announced: 10:39 A.M. Eastern Standard Time, with a half hour window (time before and after launch) for delay. During the day, Spacehab was officially declared "ready" for the mission, with all the important, essential gear stowed away. Shuttle workers closed the tunnel that connected the Spacehab to the rest of the shuttle cabin and continued stowing additional experiments (including live rodents, fish, and roundworms) in the middeck. Later that day, the communications system was activated and workers began moving the Rotating Service Structure—the protective gantry (scaffolding) that normally surrounds the shuttle while it's on the launching pad—away from *Columbia* in preparation for the launch. By nighttime, the orbiter's fuel cells were activated. These would provide the right combination of oxygen and hydrogen needed to generate the electricity that would power the shuttle and all its systems during the flight.

In the early morning hours of January 16, Launch Pad 39A was gearing up for its big day. Other than shuttle engineers, inspectors, scientists, and armed guards for security measures, the launch pad was quiet and the shuttle looked grand as it was illuminated in flood lights against the black sky. At around 3:00 A.M. the launch control team was given the go-ahead to begin filling *Columbia*'s fuel tanks.

It took a half-million gallons of fuel to fill *Columbia*'s tanks: 143,351 gallons of liquid hydrogen oxydizer and 385,285 gallons of liquid hydrogen. Fueling took nearly three hours and was finished around 6:00 A.M., just in time for inspectors to give one final look around. Armed with binoculars, telescopes, and other high-tech tools, they looked for anything that might pose a threat to the shuttle launch.

Back at what was called the "suit room," where the astronauts donned their pressurized space suits, Ilan, Rick Husband, Willie McCool, Laurel Clark, Dave Brown, Michael Anderson, and Kalpana Chawla left their quarantine quarters. Like seven bright orange walking pumpkins, they headed for the silver "astrovan" that would take them to the launch pad.

Just before loading onto the astrovan, the STS-107 crew of seven stopped to embrace as one. Commander Rick Husband led them in prayer, then in a moment of silence in memory of the *Challenger* crew who had died at that same moment 17 years before.

At T-minus three hours (Target Time—10:39 A.M.—minus three hours), security helicopters buzzed overhead, filling the skies, and ground security flooded the road leading to the Kennedy Space Center, in preparation for the arrival of the astronauts. Flags representing many nations waved among the crowd of spectators: American flags for the American astronauts, Indian flags for Kalpana Chawla's native country, India, and Israeli flags in honor of Ilan. People were passing out T-shirts and buttons bearing the smiling face of Ilan. The message on the shirts and buttons read in both English and in Hebrew: *Ilan Ramon, Israel's First Astronaut.* When the astrovan pulled up to the launch pad, a roaring cheer went up from the crowd. It was 7:45 A.M. when Ilan and the other astronauts stepped out of the silver van at the mobile launch platform and headed toward the towering shuttle, stopping to pose for photographs and wave to the crowd. Dressed in their flight suits, they smiled and blew kisses in the air before heading for the elevator that would take them up to the entrance to the shuttle.

After the short ride up, they crossed the catwalk that connected the shuttle and elevator. It was then that Commander Husband climbed through the hatch into the *Columbia* and was fastened into his commander's position in the shuttle cockpit. He was the first crew member to board. A few minutes later, the other astronauts began boarding *Columbia*. It was the responsibility of the "close-out crew" to strap the astronauts into their seats after they boarded the shuttle. Ilan was the second astronaut to board *Columbia*. Next was Willie McCool, then Michael Anderson, David Brown, Laurel Clark and, finally, Kalpana Chawla. By 9:17 A.M. all the astronauts were fastened in place and the shuttle hatch was closed. Not long after, Commander Husband made his first radio contact with Launch Control and began a series of communications checks in preparation for the launch.

At 10:00 A.M., six buses filled with Ilan's friends and family entered the Kennedy Space Center. After enduring detailed security checks at many checkpoints from the Hilton Hotel (where they were staying) to the Space Center, they joined the other astronaut families at the VIP viewing stands a few miles from the launch pad. Preparations for the launch continued and the countdown clock ticked away. Every so often, the astronauts and ground control were polled in what they referred to as a "go–no go" poll, which simply asked each crew member, one at a time, if he or she was good to "go." Anything can change in the moments before lift-off, including something traumatic enough to cancel the mission. Someone might fall ill after being strapped into the shuttle, or the weather conditions can change in an instant. But everything was still a "go."

Commander Husband's voice came over the radio into Launch Control at the Kennedy Space Center. "The Lord has blessed us with a beautiful day here," he said. He told them that the crew was ready. There would be no more delays.

At once, the crew "access arm" began to pull away from the shuttle, and auxiliary power was started. The liquid oxygen tank was pressurized. The space shuttle's three engines ignited. And at 10:39 A.M.—right on schedule—*Columbia* lifted off from the launch pad! In a deafening roar, *Columbia* soared into the sky at speeds of 1,800 miles per hour. The solid rocket boosters (attached to the orbiter to give it extra lift-off power) separated—as they were supposed to—and fell away. *Columbia* headed straight for orbit, its destination 180 miles above Earth. On the ground, Mission Control was quiet, waiting for their first communication from the STS-107 commander after the shuttle broke out of the Earth's atmosphere into space.

As part of the launch procedure, the space shuttle's main engines shut down and the giant external fuel tank attached to the orbiter section of the spacecraft separated and burned up in the atmosphere. On board, Commander Husband and Pilot McCool began the process of switching the ship over from its launching configuration to its orbiting configuration. Finally, at 11:23 A.M., the call came loud and clear from the shuttle into Mission Control: "We thank you very much, Houston," Husband told mission controllers. "We made sure we welcomed everybody to space and they're all doing great!" Everybody at Mission Control cheered.

On the ground at Cape Canaveral, everyone cheered, too. The launch of *Columbia* was a beautiful sight to behold under a perfect, clear blue sky.

In Israel, nearly every citizen sat glued to the television set to watch the launch live. Rarely has a nation been more in need of something to celebrate. With so many terrorist suicide bombings, a poor economy, and low morale, Ilan's participation on STS-107 provided them with the most exciting, happy occasion they could celebrate. "This

67

is a great moment for Israelis," Israel's Ambassador Daniel Ayalon said at the launch. "It's an achievement of excellence. We are so proud." Ambassador Ayalon also made a point of noting the bright blue and white color of the sky that day. "Those are our national colors," he said proudly.

"In Israel today," Ilan told the *Jerusalem Post* just before the flight, "there's a huge problem of economics and un-employment. This is the most important problem in Israel today. I think people are very happy to be distracted by my flight, maybe to forget a little bit of their problems and get out there with us."

Happy, indeed. "First Hebrew Astronaut Since Elijah!" cried Israel's most popular newspaper, *Yediot Achranot*. In classrooms all across the State, students and teachers hung pictures and articles about Ilan on their walls. The Israeli Postal Authority planned to issue a commemorative stamp. One mattress manufacturer even proclaimed he would name a line of mattresses after Ilan!

10

Life in Space

If I stay awake for 90 minutes after my shift, I'll see the entire globe. That's an experience of a lifetime.

Ilan Ramon, to the *Baltimore Jewish Times*

In effect, the space shuttle *Columbia* had three "rooms": the flight deck where all operations and Earth observations would place; the middeck, which included the toilet, galley (eating area), sleeping bunks, some experiments, and storage lockers; and the Spacehab module, where the majority of the experiments would be performed. Spacehab was a pressurized research module 20 feet long, 14 feet wide, and 11 feet high. It was also where much of the equipment needed for the experiments was stored, some even mounted on its roof.

The seven-member STS-107 crew was divided into two teams, each team working 12 hours per "Flight Day" during the 16-day mission. On the first day of the mission (Flight Day 1), while the Blue Team (Willie McCool, Dave Brown, and Michael Anderson) began their six-hour sleep period, the Red Team (Rick Husband, Kalpana Chawla,

Lauren Clark, and Ilan) began activating experiments in the Spacehab lab. They had a busy science schedule and there wasn't a moment to waste. After changing out of their space "pumpkin" suits and into more comfortable work clothes, they got to work.

What's life in space like for a shuttle astronaut? It is the responsibility of NASA to make sure their astronauts are safe, healthy, and comfortable during a space mission. They must make sure that tasty food is available, that there are comfortable living conditions, and that the astronauts can practice good hygiene. For a sixteen-day flight in very close quarters—and in zero gravity conditions—this presents quite a challenge.

Because of the small confines of the shuttle, astronauts must work extra hard to stay out of one another's way. For example, if the Red Team is asleep and the Blue Team is at work, the Blue Team needs to make sure it doesn't create any unnecessary noise near the bunk area. As the work space is only a few feet away from the sleeping bunks, this isn't always easy. The sleeping bunks are comprised of four alcoves directly next to one another. Each bunk is about the size of a small closet. They're all soundproofed in order to minimize noise. Ilan shared his bunk with one of the astronauts on the Blue Team, who slept during a different shift.

Astronaut food is a lot like camping food, or the food eaten by soldiers stationed in the field. These include not only supermarket products that don't need refrigeration, but also vacuum-sealed, pre-prepared meals the astronauts select from a menu before the flight. All drinks come in foil packets similar to juice packs. To drink, an astronaut injects several ounces of cold or hot water into the pack, shakes the pack to mix the contents, and then inserts a straw and sips.

Though Ilan's menu was only slightly different from his crewmates because of his kosher meals, nearly all meals were prepared in the same way: they got mixed with water and were then heated in a microwave. A typical breakfast for Ilan was Mexican scrambled eggs, a tortilla, and a granola bar. The granola bars were just opened and eaten, but the eggs came freeze-dried. After injecting them with hot water, Ilan would then open the plastic container with a scissors and eat the eggs with a spoon.

Tortillas are a favorite food among astronauts because they stay fresh for long periods of time, don't take much storage room, and best of all, make great flying saucers in zero gravity! As we saw via satellite TV during the mission, the astronauts sometimes enjoyed playing with their food before eating it. Thanks to the low gravity conditions, floating cornflakes, flying tortillas, even drops of water or juice can become fun playthings in space.

Practicing good hygiene is one of the bigger challenges the astronauts are faced with in space. They use a small hand cleaner (which produces water and then sucks it away) to wash up with, but since there is no bath or shower on the shuttle, their bodies are never fully submerged in water. They must use large wet-wipes—the kind hospitals use for bedridden patients—to clean themselves. And though brushing teeth is fairly simple, spitting out can be a problem! In order to avoid having their saliva float around the cabin in weightless globs, the astronauts must spit into a paper towel, then throw it away.

All clothes and food on the shuttle are packed very tightly to reduce the amount of space needed for storage. The same goes for dirty clothes and uneaten food. Dirty clothes go into laundry bags that are stuffed into a corner of the shuttle, and wet towels and used food containers are put into a special sealed, wet trash container to prevent odors from escaping.

Another challenge aboard the shuttle is presented when "nature calls." How do the astronauts go to the bathroom in space? Thanks to modern technology, the shuttle toilet has become very "high-tech" over the years. It's called a "Waste Containment System" and it looks a lot like the toilet you'd find on an airplane. One difference is that there are handlebars and a seat belt on the shuttle toilet to help keep the occupant in place. And instead of gravity, a strong vacuum of air pulls the waste away from the body. The solid waste is then vacuum dried and compacted, and the liquid waste is dumped overboard.

On the shuttle, everyone is responsible for cleaning up after themselves. The pilot is responsible for keeping the toilet in working order. If the toilet breaks, the astronauts must use plastic bags. During launch and landing, if an astronaut has to go to the bathroom, he or she must use an adult-sized diaper. As you can imagine, most astronauts make sure they "go" in advance of a launch or landing so they don't have to put on a diaper!

It's easy to lose track of the date in space because the shuttle orbits the Earth every 90 minutes and a "new day" begins with each orbit. To keep track of the date, the STS-107 crew used color-coded cardboard signs. "If you ask me what day it is I have no clue," Ilan said by satellite while in orbit. Instead, the crew kept track of days by the number of days they'd been on the mission. For example, January 16, the day they lifted off, was Flight Day 1; January 17 was Flight Day 2; and so on.

Most of Ilan's working shift was spent in the Spacehab module running experiments. Even when he was not working, Ilan was "working"—wearing a small watch computer on his wrist that monitored his activity level and the amount of light as part of a sleep research study. Video footage from inside Spacehab also showed Ilan riding a bicycle while connected to a breathing tube as part of a different experiment. With 80 experiments on board, there was always data to collect or reports to record.

Despite their many important space projects, the STS-107 crew made time for fun. In the pictures we saw from space, the crew was always smiling and, more often than not, laughing. They told jokes to each other or made fun of each other's wild, floating space hair. They even played with their food together. With their clipboards, high-tech tools, and research packs floating around them, they expressed joy at where they were and what they were doing. They didn't seem to take a single moment for granted.

Periodically, they spoke to us down here on Earth via satellite. They gave us video tours of the shuttle and answered our questions in live interviews. On some nights we were treated to Ilan and his friends floating around the cabin tumbling weightlessly through the air, or holding onto each other's feet, coasting through the shuttle. Ilan particularly loved to soar like a bird through the cabin. According to Ilan's wife, a sentiment later echoed by a NASA Colonel eulogizing the crew, "In space, Ilan was in his element." In fact, at one point during the mission, Ilan was asked by the flight surgeon via satellite how he felt. Ilan responded, "I am sick." The flight surgeon asked, "What's wrong?" Ilan replied jokingly, "I have ground sickness. I must stay in space longer. I cannot return to Earth."

Every day was an adventure aboard *Columbia*, but a special moment for Ilan occurred on Flight Day 8, when his Red Team was awakened by the music of his favorite Israeli singer, Arik Einstein. Ilan's wife, Rona, had asked NASA to play, "Ma ata oseh kesheata kan baboker" (What are you doing when you wake up in the morning) for the crew, as it was one of Ilan's favorite songs and it had to do with mornings. "It's nice to hear a Hebrew song up here," Ilan said.

Ilan and the astronauts spoke with many different people (politicians, students, children, news anchors, and reporters) from the space shuttle when they weren't performing experiments, and sometimes *while* they were performing experiments. During one televised video conference with the crew on Flight Day 3, a CNN (Cable News Network) anchor asked Ilan what his thoughts were as the shuttle passed over Israel. "To tell you the truth," Ilan replied, "it was pretty fast. It was partly or mostly cloudy, so I couldn't see much of Israel, just the north of Israel, and of course I was excited." He went on to add that the mission was an "opening for great science from our nation, and hopefully for all our neighbors in the Middle East."

Ilan had the opportunity to talk more about passing over Israel with Prime Minister Ariel Sharon on Flight Day 6 (January 21), in a historic teleconference that was beamed down to Israel via satellite. The prime minister spoke to Ilan from his office in Jerusalem where he had invited more than 30 guests and reporters to sit in on their conversation: "What do you see from there that we don't see from here?" the prime minister asked Ilan. "We see the Earth, which is beautiful," Ilan replied. Sharon then asked Ilan to extend his greetings to the rest of the STS-107 crew, and invited them all to visit Jerusalem in the future.

It was on Flight Day 11 (January 26) that Ilan caught the most inspiring view of Israel from the shuttle. It appeared below him so crystal clear that he could actually see Jerusalem, the state capitol. The vision affected him so greatly that he wrote an emotional e-mail to Israel's president, Moshe Katsav. Ilan's inspiring words touched a nation as soon as the e-mail was published in newspapers across Israel:

Dear Mr. President,

It's an honor and a great privilege for me to write you this letter from space. As you probably know, I blasted off to space about ten days ago on board of space shuttle *Columbia,* and by that got lucky to be the first Israeli in space.

During the last four and a half years I have been training for this mission, and after a few delays we finally made it.

As a lot of my fellow astronauts at NASA told me—it was worth the wait. The experience of being in space is something that no words can really describe and although we work 18 hours a day, we have a lot of fun and an extraordinary and exciting time.

This morning, Saturday, January 26th, we had flown over Israel, and although it wasn't the first pass, it was the best.

From space I could easily spot Jerusalem and while looking at Jerusalem, our capital, I prayed just one short prayer—*Shema Yisrael.*

I believe, as I have said a few times earlier, that we have in Israel the best people with phenomenal abilities, and it takes only the right leadership to lead the people of Israel to reach the sky!

Mr. President, if you would find it appropriate, please convey my deep appreciation to all Israel's citizens and let them know I am honored to be their first representative ever in space. In our mission we have a variety of international scientific experiments and scientists, including scientists from Arab states. We are all working this mission for the benefit of all mankind, and from space our world looks as one unity with no borders.

So let me call from up here in space—let's work our way for peace and better life for everyone on Earth.

With that I thank you, Mr. President, and send you my best blessing for a long and healthy life—to you and all your family.

Ilan Ramon

Ilan also spoke to students in classrooms around the world via satellite, doing his best to answer their questions and provide them with a taste of what life was like in space. When one student asked Ilan what he found most amazing so far about travel in space, Ilan answered that it was the feeling of weightlessness: "You don't see us float now," he told the student as he spoke from the Spacehab, "because we have to stay in front of the camera. But floating going to sleep in a little closet and floating inside it is something like the magicians show us. It really is tremendous."

Everything seemed like magic aboard the space shuttle *Columbia,* according to its astronauts. When asked to talk about amazing moments they had experienced so far, Kalpana Chawla spoke excitedly about a phenomenon that had happened to her while on the orbiter's flight deck. As a sunset overtook the view, Kalpana suddenly began to see her reflection in the overhead windows, along with the bright and dark sides of the Earth.

"In the retina of my eye, the whole Earth and sky could be seen reflected," she gushed. "So I called all the crew members one by one, and they saw it, and they all said, 'Oh, wow!'"

Astronaut Laurel Clark was also awed by what she saw as she videotaped flowers in a fragrance experiment on board. "There were roses in there, and they had been buds, and they had opened up to bloom," she said, "and it was so, so magical to see roses growing in our laboratory in space!"

On Flight Day 13, Ilan and the STS-107 crew had the rare opportunity to send their greetings to other astronauts who were also in space at the time. Commander Ken Bowersox, astronaut Don Pettit, and cosmonaut (Russian astronaut) Nikolai Budarin were aboard the International Space Station when *Columbia*'s Red Team called them.

"I wish I could stay [up here longer] like you guys," Ilan told them.

"We'd love to have you here visiting as well," Commander Bowersox replied.

The two teams of astronauts also discussed the anniversary of the *Challenger* shuttle tragedy. The astronauts that died in that 1986 accident had been colleagues of Bowersox and Pettit. Bowersox told Ilan and the members of the Red Team, that the legacy of the fallen astronauts lives on today "with a space station occupied 365 days a year, an independent shuttle program serving both the station and the broader science community, and the objectives that all those people stood for."

On one of Ilan's last days in space, he spoke passionately from the shuttle: "The world looks marvelous from up here. So peaceful, so wonderful, and so fragile. The atmosphere is so thin and fragile, and I think everybody, all of us, have to keep it clean and good. It saves our life and gives us life."

11

Coming Home

"Morning" aboard a space shuttle is very different from "morning" on Earth. Since the space shuttle makes a complete orbit around the Earth every 90 minutes, astronauts traveling aboard experience a "day" every hour and a half. The sun rises, then sets, every 90 minutes. Since it's difficult to function in a 90-minute day, the crew aboard *Columbia* kept track of time throughout their entire mission according to whatever time it was in Houston, Texas, at NASA Mission Control.

In truth, the *Columbia* crew experienced two "morning" wake-up calls in each 24-hour period during their mission. Because the shuttle's work space was so limited, the crew worked in two, 12-hour shifts to give the astronauts more room to conduct their experiments and do their work. But on Flight Day 16, the final morning of Mission STS-107, everyone aboard the shuttle had risen together. What had become the "morning" routine for the *Columbia* astronauts began shortly after their Scottish wake-up call: they brushed their teeth, washed their faces, ate a light breakfast, then began the process of checking the shuttle's many gauges to be sure everything was in order.

This routine was performed a few times, primarily for the purpose of double and triple checking for signs of trouble. They found no obvious signs of trouble. There had been a minor concern over possible damage to the shuttle's left wing during take-off 15 days before, but after extensive evaluations of video footage from the launch, it had been concluded that the damage did not pose a threat to the shuttle.

By 8:09 A.M. (Houston time), all seven astronauts were seated in place, preparing to bid farewell to the place they had called "home" for more than two weeks. A few of the astronauts e-mailed their families about the excitement they felt getting ready to return home. They also wrote about their feelings of sadness for having to end their historic mission.

The process of re-entry, or, re-entering the Earth's atmosphere, is one of the most intense, often dangerous parts of a space shuttle mission. Because of the supersonic speeds at which the shuttle needs to travel (upward of twenty-five times the speed of sound), there is great friction exerted by the air on the "skin" (metallic exterior) of the vehicle. This friction can cause temperature on the outside of the skin to become so hot that it reaches thousands of degrees. For this reason, space shuttles are built with protective foam tiles covering the entire craft. The tiles act as insulators to the body of the shuttle.

The entire process of re-entry takes nearly six hours to complete, and everything inside the shuttle must be in place in order to begin. Early on, the crew members shimmied out of their sleep restraints, stowed their gear to prevent it from moving about the cabin during the bumpy flight, and belted themselves into their seats. For the trip, each crew member wore a space helmet and donned his or her pressurized "pumpkin" suit.

Mission Commander Rick Husband, William McCool, Kalpana Chawla, and Laurel Clark sat together in the cockpit. Michael Anderson, David Brown, and Ilan sat in a small compartment beneath the cockpit. For Anderson, Brown, and Ilan, there was very little to do during the re-entry and the trip home. Their "job" was pretty much to sit quietly, leaving the airwaves clear for the pilots to communicate with Mission Control. Ilan, in particular, was excited for the opportunity to sit back, relax, and take in his last views of space.

Rick Husband and William McCool would be the busiest crew members during the shuttle's re-entry. They were to communicate with Mission Control in Houston while also monitoring the ship's series of computer-generated maneuvers on their consoles. As the spacecraft flew, they watched an image of the shuttle on their consoles as it rocked back and forth. This process, called a "roll reversal," is how a space shuttle goes about consuming excess energy so it can slow from its orbiting speed of 18,000 miles per hour to 225 miles per hour.

In the beginning, re-entry for *Columbia* was uneventful. At 8:15 A.M., while the ship flew high over the Indian Ocean, Commander Rick Husband fired his de-orbit engines (to force the shuttle out of its Earth-circling orbit), which was part of the usual procedure. Half an hour later, *Columbia* reached the edges of the Earth's atmosphere—just north of Hawaii, at an altitude of about 400,000 feet.

The astronauts were almost home.

12

Columbia is Lost

The clock ticked and we counted, and it was quiet when we should have heard a noise. There were supposed to be sonic booms, but they didn't come. That raised some concern. Then [NASA officials] took us from [the viewing stands]. They said they didn't know anything. But we knew everything.

Rona Ramon, February 1 (*People* magazine)

The reunions were ready and the celebrations were waiting at the Kennedy Space Center where *Columbia* was due to land. Back in Israel, Israelis again were sitting by their televisions, waiting to watch their hero come home. But when the countdown clock in Florida started counting *up* after touchdown time had come and gone, it became apparent that something had happened to *Columbia*. Anxiously the world waited to hear reports that the shuttle had landed, but there was nothing. Slowly, the realization began to sink in. There would be no "Welcome Home" party for Ilan and the crew of STS-107.

Over Texas, the quiet winter morning was shattered by a series of sonic booms as pieces of the crumbling spacecraft fell from the atmosphere and rained over the countryside. The news spread quickly as millions watched the images of an exploding space shuttle appear on their televisions. It was a sight many could not bear to witness. Once it became clear that *Columbia* would not be landing, the families of the astronauts were escorted by NASA representatives from Cape Canaveral and flown to Houston where a psychologist and a NASA representative were assigned to each family. Rona Ramon and her children sought comfort from close family friend, astronaut Steve MacLean.

MacLean, who went into space aboard *Columbia* eleven years before, had helped Ilan through his entire training at NASA. He and his wife had become close with the Ramons, and after hearing about the tragedy, he rushed to be by their side. NASA was thankful for the MacLeans and their close relationship to Rona, as they realized that an experienced astronaut, who knew the ins and outs of space travel, could be more helpful than a psychologist during the stressful period after a disaster.

Also by Rona's side was Brigadier General Ra'anan Falk, an Air Force attaché in Washington, D.C., who was also an old friend of the Ramon family. He and Ilan had gone through pilot training together back in Israel, and the two had remained close friends. Brig. Gen. Falk stayed with the Ramons in Houston to offer solace to the grief-stricken family.

Israel's Ambassador Ayalon traveled to Houston with the Ramon family as well. Rona told him about her last conversation with Ilan, which had taken place three days before. "He told her how beautiful the universe was," Ayalon told *Ha'Aretz*, "and how much he felt part of this universe." Rona also said that Ilan would now be part of the universe of which he was so in awe.

"Ilan departed when he was at the peak of his career," Rona later told fellow mourners. "He was with the people he loved and in a place he enjoyed so much. We will carry on his will of life," she added. "He had a smile, and we will carry on that smile."

Colonel Ilan Ramon and his family had planned to head back to Israel, to the house he and his wife were building in Ramat Gan, as soon as his work at the Space Center was finished. He'd hoped to be back in time for son Tal's *Bar Mitzvah*. He'd hoped to retire for real and enjoy life in his homeland with his wife and four children. He'd hoped to play squash and go snow-skiing again—two of his favorite pastimes. He'd also hoped to write a book about his experiences as an Israeli astronaut, preparations for which he had already discussed with his close friend and fellow author, Rabbi Daniel Gordis. Rona and her children would now return to Israel without husband and father.

As the Jewish world mourned Ilan, it also paid tribute to his life in many ways. After his death, people came to understand what a remarkably kind person he was and the enormous impact he had had on a whole nation. They began to learn about the fascinating, final five years of his life as he prepared and conducted research experiments among the stars, the results of which might one day save human lives. Even now they continue to celebrate the remarkable connection he had with his six crew mates—from different religions and nationalities—and how they all came to love one another and work side by side in peace for the betterment of mankind.

Months later, it was determined by NASA investigators that the piece of foam that had become dislodged from the shuttle's skin upon take-off had indeed done enough damage to the left wing of the shuttle to cause the accident. While that information does little to ease the great sorrow felt by the mourning families of the astronauts, they are comforted by the fact that we can learn from the tragedy of *Columbia* and hopefully prevent it from ever happening again.

13

Fallen Stars

When *Columbia* disintegrated over Texas, it took with it:

- A former U.S. Air Force colonel and fighter jock who loved to dress up in his spacesuit at Halloween and pose for pictures with the children at his church in Houston: Commander Rick Husband.

- A distinguished Navy pilot who enjoyed more than anything backpacking in the mountains with his wife and sons: Pilot Willie McCool.

- A veteran African-American astronaut making his second trip into space, who'd dreamed of becoming an astronaut as a young boy and who'd been an avid *Star Trek* fan: Payload Commander Mike Anderson.

- An Indian-born woman with a Ph.D. who enjoyed flying aerobatics and who established a program that brought two students from her former school in India to NASA space school every year, and cooked Indian foods for them so they wouldn't feel homesick: Mission Specialist Kalpana Chawla.

- A medical doctor who had once performed in the circus as an acrobat, and who adored his golden retriever, Duggins: Mission Specialist Dave Brown.

- Another doctor, a wife and mother, who was also an avid scuba diver and parachutist, whom friends nick-named "Floral" because of her vibrant, colorful personality: Mission Specialist Laurel Clark.
- And an Israeli Air Force hero who had helped change history twice in his life: once, after flying on a dangerous mission over enemy territory to destroy an Iraqi nuclear reactor, and again by being the first Israeli to ever see Israel from space.

As U.S. President Bush told a shocked nation just hours after the tragedy: "The same Creator who names the stars also knows the names of the seven souls we mourn today."

At a cabinet meeting in Jerusalem, Prime Minister Ariel Sharon—who had spoken with Ilan in that televised broadcast just days before—addressed his cabinet: "From the moment that we learned of the loss of contact," Sharon said solemnly, "we followed, together with the rest of the citizens of the world, in trepidation, hope and prayer, the updates which reached us from the Space Agency until the bitter moment when there was no doubt that the seven astronauts were killed in the space shuttle explosion. I wish to send from here, on behalf of the government and people of Israel, our sincere condolences to the families of the American astronauts, to the President of the United States, George Bush, and to the people of the United States.

"Times such as these strengthen the bonds of our common fate, values and vision, all of which were realized in Colonel Ilan Ramon's journey into space. Unfortunately,

I did not get to know Ilan as well as I would have wished. But I know about his past as a bold fighter pilot and an outstanding commander. I spoke to Ilan a number of times before he took off on his last mission, and I spoke to him while he was on board. In my conversations with Ilan, I recognized a man of values. A man who dearly loved his people and country. A man who did not deserve to be taken from us, along with our hopes, dreams, history and future, to a place beyond that which we could ever have imagined."

Sharon added that the seven astronauts killed were part of the heavy price paid by the human race in its quest for knowledge. "Man's journey into space will continue," he said. "Cooperation between the United States and Israel in this field will also continue. The day will come when we will launch more Israeli astronauts into space. I am sure that each and every one of them will carry in his heart the memory of Ilan Ramon, a pioneer in Israeli space travel. All the people of Israel bow their heads in memory of Colonel Ramon and the crew of the space shuttle *Columbia*, heroes of manned space flight."

Ilan's remains were sent by plane to Israel for burial. By the request of his family, Ilan would be laid to rest in a civilian cemetery in Moshav Nahalal, near where Ilan had trained as a pilot, and where the Ramons had many dear friends, rather than in Israel's military cemetery in Jerusalem. The Ramon family preferred the cemetery at Nahalal because it was more private and had many lovely trees.

It was a dreary, rainy afternoon on February 10 when Israel's fallen astronaut arrived at Lod Air Force Base outside Tel Aviv, accompanied by seven United States,

European, and Canadian astronauts as a sort of international honor guard. In a quiet hangar at the air base, Ilan's coffin was draped in the blue-and-white flag of Israel as hundreds of politicians, soldiers, diplomats and clergy, family and friends looked on. Even the schoolchildren who had designed some of Ilan's space experiments were in attendance. The sounds of a saxophone could be heard, as the song, "Can you hear my voice, O my love from afar," played softly, the same music Rona had asked NASA to play for one of Ilan's wake-up calls during the mission.

"This is not how you imagined we all imagined your homecoming," said Prime Minster Sharon. "Ilan, the son of a mother who survived the Holocaust, and a father who is a veteran of the War of Independence, was a courageous combat pilot and an outstanding officer, and was among the best of our sons and warriors. On his last mission, he soared higher than any other Israeli, and realized his dream."

Sharon then spoke directly to Rona, Assaf, Tal, Yiftach, and five-year-old Noa. "The pain you suffer is the pain we all suffer," he told them. "Ilan has touched the hidden spot in every Jew's heart. His youthful face, his eternal smile, his fresh countenance, the twinkle in his eyes penetrated our souls."

President Moshe Katsav recalled Ilan's e-mail, which had been written only days before. He told the mourners that Ilan became a Jewish international hero, not just because he participated in the shuttle mission, but because of his decision to honor Jewish heritage in space. He also said that Ilan symbolized the deep connection between Israel and the United States. "The Star of David, the blue and white of our flag, were interwoven with the American Stars and Stripes, and the common fate of the team poignantly strengthened the staunch partnership between our nations."

Noa Ramon sat nestled in her mother's arms during most of the ceremony, letting go only when Rona and her oldest son, Assaf, rose to read an e-mail they'd received from astronaut Dave Brown. In the e-mail, Ilan's crewmate spoke about a letter Ilan had given him to read on the shuttle. It had been a letter from a Holocaust survivor whose 7-year-old daughter didn't survive. "I was stunned that such a beautiful planet could harbor such awful things," Dave Brown wrote to the Ramons. When Assaf finished reading, he and his mother delicately touched Ilan's coffin before returning to their seats.

Air Force Major General Dan Halutz—the colleague who called Ilan back in 1997 to tell him he'd been chosen to become an astronaut—read aloud an Air Force poem that concluded with the words, "Bring the pilot's soul to land safely on the runway of eternal rest."

When the ceremony was over, the coffin was carried back out into the rain to a waiting military vehicle flanked by eight Israeli Air Force pilots. The family followed, Noa still holding on tightly to her mother's hand, as the words of Israel's president still rang in their ears and in their hearts: "Here one person was able, in his final days, in his short life, from the strength of his personality, to unite all the different parts of the Jewish people."

14

Remembering a Hero

Ilan's grave at the cemetery in Nahalal has since become a spot visited by hundreds of people each day. It is reported that nearly every Israeli has made the trip to Nahalal since the funeral. Ilan's gravesite is situated right next to the gravesite of former Prime Minister Moshe Dayan, and among the sites of many early Israeli heroes and settlers. An article in the Israeli newspaper *Ma'Ariv* said it was an appropriate site for Israel's fallen astronaut: "They were the first to come to Israel, and he was the first to go into space."

Jews around the world, in an outpouring of emotion, have paid tribute to Ilan in many different ways. Parks, schools, and streets have been named in honor and in memory of Colonel Ramon, and playgrounds, such as the Ilan Ramon Space Play Park in Beersheva, have been built to provide the children of Israel an educational, fun way to play, while also learning about their fallen hero.

Israel will be much greener since Ilan's passing, too, as thousands of new trees have been planted in his memory. While Ilan was in space, he called upon every Jew in the world to plant a tree in the coming year. "I would like to see at least 13 or 14 million new trees planted in Israel," he said from orbit. When he died, it seemed fitting that

Jews honor his request, which they have been doing ever since February 1, 2003.

Other memorials to the *Columbia* crew include one in Jerusalem's Independence Park, near where a memorial already stands to the astronauts who perished in the *Challenger* tragedy in 1986. And in August 2003, seven asteroids circling the sun between the orbits of Mars and Jupiter were named for Ilan and the STS-107 crew, after NASA proposed honoring the astronauts. That proposal was approved by the International Astronomical Union, and the data naming the asteroids has officially since been recorded.

Israel's Holocaust Museum in Jerusalem, Yad Vashem, prepared a special exhibit to honor the memory of Colonel Ramon. The exhibit includes photographs of Ilan and of Petr Gintz, the young boy killed in the Holocaust whose drawing Ilan took into space. Also on display is a Page of Testimony, which had been filled out years before by Ilan's mother, Tonia, for her father, Izchak Kreppel, whom she lost in the Holocaust.

While *Columbia* is gone, its mission continues. The legacy of the seven astronauts will live on forever.

EULOGIES FOR
COLONEL ILAN RAMON

FEBRUARY 11, 2003, NAHALAL CEMETERY
CHIEF OF THE GENERAL STAFF'S EULOGY FOR
ILAN RAMON

We have come to this valley to bid you farewell, Ilan.

We have all come here, to the last station of a long journey, a very long journey. A journey lasting thousands of years and another 16 days.

We have come here, Ilan, and with us is your father, Eliezer Wolfermann, your wife, Rona, your children—Assaf, Tal, Yiftach, and Noa—your family, commanders, and your friends.

Also here with us today, accompanying you with their hearts, are millions of Israelis, Jews and friends from home and from around the world, sharing memories and images, of you, like small pieces of a mosaic belonging to a larger picture. You brought together Jews from all walks of life, beliefs and symbols.

From the origins of pain and suffering, from the story of your mother Tonia, a Holocaust survivor and of your father's escape from Nazi Germany to Israel where he partook in the establishment of the Jewish State. Your life binds together the past and the future, dreams with reality.

With you, it was as if you carried the state of Israel, the IDF and the whole Jewish nation—stations of life, the Holocaust and the rebirth of Israel.

A whole nation breathlessly followed your journey.

For sixteen days, we offered forth our prayers, not only those to IDF soldiers in the air, sea and on the ground, but also to you in space.

The State of Israel basked in your happiness, joy and excitement, and in the end was left with pain and sorrow, a bitter and fervent pain.

As a song of praise by Mordechai Zaira says:

You accompanied me, my land, with your white
   almond trees
with the radiance of your anger and the vastness of
   your fields,
and you sang the song of praise,
to sound it far, far from your borders.

Thus you felt and thus we felt, accompanying you far from our borders on a mission whose words and melody you composed into a song of praise.

We have lost you Ilan, and in the same breath, thanks to you, we have rediscovered the most important source of our strength, our unity.

Our mission, to defend the State of Israel, requires great dedication, body and soul.

You were a dedicated combat pilot, astronaut and citizen of the State of Israel—always accompanied by a strong sense of a deep and solid National Jewish identity. You gave us the hope that we could find all that is good and beautiful in the people of this land.

A pilot, fighter and scientist. You logged thousands of hours flight time in which you defended the borders of the State of Israel. For 30 years you were one of the best pilots and you participated in one of the most important missions in the history of the IDF, operation "Opera." Even then, as the youngest in the group, you outdid yourself during the bombing of the Iraqi nuclear reactor. You and your friends broke the limits of what was possible and you gave the state of Israel and the world breathing space, security and stability.

These days, however, Iraq still poses a real threat to the State of Israel and to world peace. Even our great friend, the USA, knows that without that historic mission, this threat would be far greater. The true friendship that exists between Israel and the USA has received today, thanks to you, a new meaning and a new depth of great importance to us.

Through you, we got to know your family, celebrated with them in their moments of joy and commiserated with them in moments of pain: Your father's great inner strength, Rona's strength, and the children's love. Beyond the grief, we have seen your loving family, who strengthen us with their radiating strength. We understand where you came from.

You bequeathed to us the faith in the Jewish nation and the Israeli society, the faith in the just way and the things that are beyond the horizon. Your diligence, the need to strive for excellence, and the will and strength not to break down even when the road is long and full of obstacles. Your infinite curiosity, determination and responsibility. You did not sway from your mission and were a great family man—all this in one person—whose dream is our dream, and whose death is our bereavement.

Rona and the children, Eliezer, Gadi, family members and friends, we will stand tall beside you on your difficult mission—the mission of resuming your lives. Let the IDF be your comfort. Let the progress of the State of Israel comfort you.

This place, where the Jewish pioneers redeemed the land, here in Nahalal that has recently celebrated its 80th anniversary, this is where your loved ones chose to have your final place of rest.

The Israeli space program, for which you served as a pioneer, will continue and I know that this would please you.

We say farewell on behalf of the Israel Defense Forces.

On behalf of the IDF, I salute you one last time.

Rest in peace, fighter.

Rest in peace, dreamer.

May your memory be blessed.

FEBRUARY 11, 2003, NAHALAL CEMETERY
ISRAEL AIR FORCE COMMANDER'S EULOGY FOR
COL. ILAN RAMON

Ilan, the man we loved to love, the best we have.

Friend, fighter and commander.

We are here in the Yizreel Valley, bidding you farewell for the last time.

Thirty of your forty-eight years you spent in military service dedicated to the people of Israel.

You withstood the difficult challenges of this land; you defended your right to fight, to be at the forefront.

Five years have passed since you were chosen to be the first Israeli astronaut. Years replete with training and studying, years of yearning to blast off into space. Five years in which you transformed in everybody's eyes to become what you always were and always will be in our eyes.

You were a modest and pleasant man, who smiled from the depth of his heart and who took upon himself to be an envoy of the Jewish people. A first class professional. A ray of light shining through our painful reality, the Israeli dream.

We all searched for a symbol to be proud of and to cling to—Ilan, you were that symbol.

We all counted down to your blast off: ten, nine, eight—to one, and you went forth from this world with power that knows no limit. Sixteen days that raised our spirits and made our hearts swell with pride.

You described it best in your own words when you said "I was in space and paved a path and new horizons for our Air Force, which is one of the most exciting things to happen in my life. It is a great honor for me to have been a member of the IAF for over 30 years and it is an honor to represent you here in space. Air and space, they are one."

We sat ready for your return waiting to see you walk, emerging from the shuttle together with your friends, expecting to see that same wide smile. We found ourselves counting back, wanting to stop the clock counting the passing seconds and minutes, revealing the harsh truth.

Ilan, you opened an opening to worlds we did not know, you swept many with your enthusiasm; you enchanted all.

On your last journey, you took the symbols of the Jewish people over the generations, the old and the new. A Bible and a mezuzah, a picture from the Holocaust and an Israel Air Force flag. You represented the State of Israel and were the envoy of the Jewish people. You saw it as a prerogative but also as a duty, which you filled with dedication.

We, your friends in the Israel Air Force, will continue to march along the path you paved, to wave the flag you waved, the flag of technological progress, the flag of excellence.

Rona, Assaf, Tal, Yiftach, Noa, Eliezer, Gadi and family members: your Ilan is our Ilan, Ilan of the Israel Air Force, who symbolizes all we want to be, Ilan who transformed the dream of many of us to his—to our—reality.

His memory will remain with us for eternity. We are always with you.

In the name of the Israel Air Force, I salute you.

Farewell Friend.

RESOURCES

For more information about Colonel Ilan Ramon, space-flight, Mission STS-107, the Israeli Air Force, NASA, or Israel, to plant a tree in memory of Colonel Ramon, or to send a message to the Ramon family, please check some of the following sources:

National Air and Space Agency (NASA) *www.NASA.gov*

NASA Headquarters, 300 E St. SW, Washington, D.C.

www.shuttlepresskit.com/STS-107

www.spaceflight.NASA.gov

www.Floridatoday.com/news/space

www.space.com

Johnson Space Center, Houston, Texas 77058

Kennedy Space Center, Spaceport USA, KSC, Florida 32899-0001

Israel Defense Forces (IDF) *www.IDF.il/newsite/english/main.stm*

The Ramon Family—*ilanfamily@mail.IDF.il*

Israel Air Force (IAF)—*www.IAF.org.il*

Israel Air Force Museum, Army Post 02832, Hatzerim, Beer-sheva, ISRAEL—*www.fai.org/education/museums/isr_mus.htm*

Israel Science & Technology Homepage—*www.science.co.il*

Israel's Ministry of Science and Technology—*www.most. gov.il/eng/*

Israel Space Agency—*www.NASA.proj.ac.il*

Tel Aviv University, Ramat Aviv, Tel Aviv, ISRAEL 69978—*www.TAU.ac.il*

The Jewish National Fund—*www.JNF.org*—1-888-JNF-0099

GLOSSARY

access arm: One of three swing arms (retracted before takeoff) that provides services or access to the space shuttle while it is waiting to be launched.

aliyah: To move to Israel (literally means "going up").

bulkhead: A structural partition used to divide an aircraft into separate compartments.

Cessna: The name of a company that manufactures small private aircraft.

cryogenic fuel storage tanks: Tanks used aboard the space shuttle to hold liquid fuel at sub-freezing temperatures so it will take up less space.

Eretz Yisra'el: The land or country of Israel.

fuselage: The central body of an aircraft to which the wings and tail assembly are attached.

kibbutz: A communal settlement in Israel where all property is shared equally by residents and committees govern all aspects of community life.

Kiddush: A blessing over wine that is said before meals on *Shabbat* and Jewish holidays.

Kiddush Cup: A special wine cup that is used to say *Kiddush*.

mezuzah: A small case that Jews hang on their doorposts containing a copy of the Hebrew text of passages in the Book of Deuteronomy.

middeck: A part of the space shuttle that serves as a partition between the pressurized and unpressurized portions of the spacecraft.

moshav: A cooperative settlement in Israel where each family owns its own land and home, and individuals make private decisions concerning work and family matters.

Page of Testimony: A document that commemorates the name and biographical details of a Jew who perished in the Holocaust.

Palestine: The former name of the land that is now Israel, before the State of Israel was created in 1948.

reflexology: A method of physical manipulation that relieves nervous tension through the application of finger pressure.

17th of Tammuz: The 17th day of the Hebrew month of Tammuz (a day of fasting) that starts the three weeks of mourning before Tisha be-Av.

Shabbat: The Hebrew name for the Jewish Sabbath.

shah: Title given to the ruler of Iran.

shaliach: Someone sent as a representative or messenger for Israel.

Shavuot: The Jewish harvest holiday that celebrates Moses' receiving the Ten Commandments.

Shema Yisra'el: An important prayer in Judaism declaring that there is only one God.

thermostabilized food: food that is unaffected by heat and can be stored safely at room temperature.

Tisha be-Av: The ninth day of the Hebrew month of Av (a day of mourning) that commemorates many of the tragedies that have befallen the Jewish people, primarily the destruction of the First and Second Temples in Jerusalem.

Torah: The five Books of Moses, the first five books of the Hebrew Bible.

zero gravity: The state or condition of weightlessness.

IMPORTANT DATES

1935   Eliezer Wolfermann leaves Nazi Germany for Palestine and settles in Tel Aviv.

1945   Tonia Kreppel is liberated from Auschwitz. She heads for Palestine but is sent to Cypress, Turkey.

1948   Israel is declared a Jewish state.

1949   Tonia Kreppel immigrates to Israel.

1949   Eliezer Wolfermann and Tonia Kreppel marry.

1952   Gadi Wolfermann (Ramon) is born.

1954   Ilan Wolfermann (Ramon) is born on June 20, near Tel Aviv.

1962   Ilan's family moves to Beersheva.

1972   Ilan graduates Makif Gimel High School and enters pilot training school at Hatzerim Air Force Base, near Beersheva. He changes his name to Ilan Ramon.

1973   Ilan serves in the Yom Kippur War.

1974   Ilan graduates pilot school and enlists in the Israeli Air Force.

1980   Ilan trains to fly the F-16 in Ogden, Utah, United States.

1981   Ilan participates in "Operation Opera," an IAF attack on a nuclear reactor in Iraq. Ilan receives a medal of honor.

1982 Ilan serves in "Operation Peace For Galilee" and receives his second medal of honor.

1983–1987 Ilan studies electronics and computer engineering at Tel Aviv University.

1986 Ilan marries Rona Bar Simantov.

1988 Ilan re-enlists in the Israeli Air Force.

1988 Ilan's and Rona's son Assaf is born.

1990 Ilan's and Rona's son Tal is born.

1993 Ilan's and Rona's son Yiftach is born.

1994 Ilan is promoted to colonel and put in charge of weapons development.

1997 Ilan is selected to become Israel's first astronaut.

1998 The Ramon family moves to Houston, Texas, United States on June 6.

1999 Ilan's and Rona's daughter Noa is born.

2001 Ilan and the STS-107 crew join the National Outdoor Leadership School for an 11-day journey together through the Rocky Mountains.

January 12, 2003
Astronauts enter quarantine.

January 16, 2003
Columbia lifts off.

January 21, 2003
Historic press conference while in orbit with Israel's prime minister, Ariel Sharon.

January 26, 2003
Ilan has the best view of Israel and sends a historic e-mail to Israel's president, Moshe Katsav.

January 28, 2003
The STS-107 crew communicates with astronauts from the International Space Station.

February 1, 2003
    Columbia is lost.

February 5, 2003
    NASA Payload Specialist Colonel Ilan Ramon's remains are identified.

February 10, 2003
    Ilan's coffin arrives at Lod Air Force Base. He is remembered in a memorial service attended by family, friends, and Israeli government and military officials.

February 11, 2003
    Colonel Ilan Ramon is laid to rest at Nahalal Cemetery.

INDEX

LaVergne, TN USA
05 May 2010
181512LV00004B/30/A